▶ ## An Information Technology Surrogate for Religion

DOI: 10.1057/9781137490599.0001

Contemporary Religion and Popular Culture

Series Editors: **A. David Lewis**, MCPHS University, USA and **Eric Mazur**, Virginia Wesleyan College, USA

The *Contemporary Religion and Popular Culture* series renews the engagement between religious studies and media studies, anthropology, literary studies, art history, musicology, philosophy, and all manner of high-level systems that undergird the everyday and commercial. Specifically, CRPC looks to upset the traditional approach to such topics by delivering top-grade scholarly material in smaller, more focused, and more digestible chunks, aiming to be the wide-access niche for scholars to further pursue specific avenues of their study that might not be supported elsewhere.

The division between high and low culture in Anglo-American environments has gradually become recognized as arbitrary, but discussion and dialogue about the wealth to be found in subgenres of music, within mall culture, through webcomics, by means of baseball sabremetrics, around adolescent fashion, on streaming video, has had a home only on the fringe. From the perspective of religious content and context, CRPC promises serious examination of topics today that will be taken all the more seriously tomorrow.

Titles include:

William Sims Bainbridge
AN INFORMATION TECHNOLOGY SURROGATE FOR RELIGION
The Veneration of Deceased Family in Online Games

DOI: 10.1057/9781137490599.0001

palgrave▶pivot

An Information Technology Surrogate for Religion: The Veneration of Deceased Family in Online Games

▶

William Sims Bainbridge

palgrave
macmillan

DOI: 10.1057/9781137490599.0001

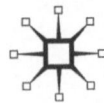

First published in 2014 by
PALGRAVE MACMILLAN®
in the United States—a division of St. Martin's Press LLC,
175 Fifth Avenue, New York, NY 10010.

Where this book is distributed in the UK, Europe and the rest of the world,
this is by Palgrave Macmillan, a division of Macmillan Publishers Limited,
registered in England, company number 785998, of Houndmills,
Basingstoke, Hampshire RG21 6XS.

Palgrave Macmillan is the global academic imprint of the above companies
and has companies and representatives throughout the world.

Palgrave® and Macmillan® are registered trademarks in the United States,
the United Kingdom, Europe and other countries

ISBN: 978–1–137–49060–5 EPUB
ISBN: 978–1–137–49059–9 PDF
ISBN: 978–1–137–49054–4 Hardback

Library of Congress Cataloging-in-Publication Data is available from
the Library of Congress.

A catalogue record of the book is available from the British Library.

First edition: 2014

www.palgrave.com/pivot

DOI: 10.1057/9781137490599

Contents

Preface

> AVA: Ancestor Veneration Avatar or Avatar for Virtual Awakening, the experience of operating an avatar based on a deceased person inside a computer-generated virtual environment.

Many innovative forms of online communication are revolutionizing human social life, as blogs and tweets shape political discourse, mobile devices link businesses nearby in the real world to their websites in cyberspace, while bookstores vanish from the landscape as online stores quickly deliver any traditional volumes, and literature itself migrates into electronic forms. In parallel, culture is changing, as for example greater awareness of diversity allows people with traditionally unfashionable religious views to "come out of the closet," and educated classes in many nations are becoming secularized. In this context, the difference between mythology and theology fades. For many people Christianity, Judaism, and Islam join Classical Paganism among the creative literary traditions of the past that are cherished but not followed. Citizens no longer have the obligation to believe the faith of the nation, but neither are they required to disbelieve, so people with a great variety of orientations toward religion experience its digital manifestations.

Among the richest of these new virtual universes is the galaxy of virtual worlds, most of which are currently marketed as massively multiplayer online (MMO) games. More than mere games, they are works of art, often combining literature, music, and visual arts comparable to

DOI: 10.1057/9781137490599.0002

motion pictures, in a novel dynamic manner that allows people to act within them through what are commonly called *avatars*, and to take a great variety of roles. The fact that *avatar*, a term from Hindu religion, was adopted by computer science as the standard term for digital representations of people hints at the possibility that information technology offers a form of transcendence. Many virtual worlds depict religion, whether as solid cathedrals where one may conduct rituals, or as fluid cults of enemies who must be destroyed.[1]

Secularization of public culture has eroded traditional reactions to death, opening room for a diversity of novel innovations.[2] This book offers ideas about how to develop avatars based on deceased persons as instruments of human spiritual advancement, and ancestor veneration, as well as tools of empirical research. It will also survey the variety of unconventional religious and magical expressions found in these game-worlds, selecting ten of them because their variety illustrates a range of general possibilities likely to be significant for all future virtual worlds, at least in the next several years. It will do so through three themes that are significant for the social science of popular culture:

1 *Methodological:* This will have some of the qualities of an instructional manual introducing methodology that both social scientists and civilian explorers can use to gain the maximum intellectually and emotionally, not only within virtual worlds, but also in structurally similar but computationally different modes of online communication. The core principles are participant observation and ethnography, and the context highlights the difference between these two sociological and anthropological methods. Participant observation requires the researcher to experience life inside the virtual world personally, not only gaining distinctive insights that can be refined into hypotheses, but also reflecting upon the personal feelings stimulated by actions and events. Ethnography documents the culture of the world, which in this area largely means the creations of the game designers, as they constructed "fictional" societies and religions. The author is experienced using these methodologies sociologically in studying unconventional religious movements in non-Internet contexts, and has been developing online methodologies over the past decade, as a program director in the Directorate for Computer and Information Science and Engineering at the National Science Foundation.[3]

DOI: 10.1057/9781137490599.0002

2   *Spiritual:* This will present a new way in which information
     technology may act as a surrogate for traditional religion in
     performing one of the key psychological functions that sacred
     mythologies played in previous centuries: adjustment to the
     deaths of loved ones. In the field often called *human-centered
     computing*, there is a good deal of scientific literature about
     how avatars relate, psychologically and socially, to their users.
     In particular the *proteus* theory holds that users can become
     their avatar to an extent sufficient to render that avatar highly
     influential on the mind of the user.[4] Human-centered computing
     combines social and cognitive science with computer and
     information science, with the goal not merely of understanding
     how people use existing technologies, but to invent new
     technologies. From that engineering perspective, developing
     ancestor veneration avatars (AVAs) presents a number of
     challenges having both technical and psychological aspects,
     including how a particular virtually resurrected individual might
     fit into a particular gameworld. The idea of AVAs was presented
     in general terms in two previous books by the author, *The Warcraft
     Civilization* and *eGods: Faith versus Fantasy in Computer Gaming*,
     and he is now ready to offer systematic methods and design
     principles.[5]

3   *Theoretical:* In the 1980s, in collaboration with leading sociologist
     of religion, Rodney Stark, the author developed a social exchange
     theory of religion.[6] Later work by the author built upon this
     systematic theoretical perspective, focusing on the two opposed
     processes of religious movements and secularization.[7] A more
     advanced study was based on neural network computer simulations
     that tested the rigor of formalized theoretical statements about
     religion, *God from the Machine: Artificial Intelligence Models of
     Religious Cognition*.[8] That last book was published in a Cognitive
     Science series and reflected the convergence of the social exchange
     theory of religion with that new discipline that emerged since the
     theory was first stated. Role-playing can be viewed rigorously in
     terms of mental frames that one person uses to model the cognition
     and behavior of another.

Integrating all three themes in the context of a specific simulated world
requires one to have considerable insight into the life and character of

another person, as well as the motivation to invest the effort necessary to collect and digest more information about that individual and his or her socio-cultural context. This project is intended to systematize this developing theoretical orientation and empirical methodology, through role-playing 11 people of significance to the author—just as others using the methodology would role-play individuals significant to themselves. There can be no doubt that this is a radically new research methodology, although it bears some superficial similarity to the *psychodrama* approach introduced decades ago by psychologist Jacob Moreno.[9] Yet the new information technologies are themselves revolutionary, and they were used to collect historical information, as well as create the avatars.

I wrote the book very much with the reader in mind, aware that different readers may have various goals, such as: (1) Learning how they themselves can use computer-generated avatars for personal, spiritual purposes. (2) Providing colleagues in the social science of religion and related fields with new research methods and theoretical concepts, with which to understand not only virtual worlds but also many other emerging features of the post-industrial Information Society. (3) Identifying design principles that programmers and other computer professionals may use to create new social technologies. (4) Raising new questions, and discovering them in the gameworlds, that concern the general meaning of human life—thus fundamentally religious, philosophical, or artistic in nature.

Notes

1   Robert M. Geraci, *Virtually Sacred: Myth and Meaning in World of Warcraft and Second Life* (New York: Oxford University Press, 2014).
2   John W. Riley, Jr, "Dying and the Meanings of Death: Sociological Inquiries," *Annual Review of Sociology*, 1983, 9: 191–216; Phyllis Palgi and Henry Abramovitch, "Death: A Cross-Cultural Perspective," *Annual Review of Anthropology*, 1984, 13: 385–417; Michael J. Kearl, "The Proliferation of Postselves in American Civic and Popular Cultures," *Mortality*, 2010, 15(1): 47–63.
3   William Sims Bainbridge, *Satan's Power: A Deviant Psychotherapy Cult* (Berkeley: University of California Press, 1978); *The Endtime Family: Children of God* (Albany, New York: State University of New York Press, 2002).

DOI: 10.1057/9781137490599.0002

4   Robert Jay Lifton, "Protean Man," *Archives of General Psychiatry*, 1971, 24(4): 298–304; Nick Yee, Jeremey Bailenson, and Nicolas Ducheneaut, "The Proteus Effect: Implications of Transformed Digital Self-Representation on Online and Offline Behavior," *Communication Research*, 2009, 36(2): 285–312; Jim Blascovich and Jeremy Bailenson, *Infinite Reality: The Hidden Blueprint of our Virtual Lives* (New York: William Morrow, 2011); Dmitri Williams, Tracy L. M. Kennedy, and Robert J. Moore, "Behind the Avatar: The Patterns, Practices, and Functions of Role Playing in MMOS," *Games and Culture*, 2011, 6(2): 171–200; *Nick Yee, The Proteus Paradox* (New Haven, CT: Yale University Press, 2014).

5   William Sims Bainbridge, *The Warcraft Civilization* (Cambridge, Massachusetts: MIT Press, 2010); *eGods: Faith Versus Fantasy in Computer Gaming* (New York: Oxford University Press, 2013).

6   Rodney Stark and William Sims Bainbridge, *The Future of Religion* (Berkeley: University of California Press, 1985); *A Theory of Religion* (New York: Toronto/ Lang, 1987); *Religion, Deviance and Social Control* (New York: Routledge, 1996).

7   William Sims Bainbridge, *The Sociology of Religious Movements* (New York: Routledge, 1997); *Across the Secular Abyss* (Lanham, Maryland: Lexington, 2007).

8   William Sims Bainbridge, *God from the Machine: Artificial Intelligence Models of Religious Cognition* (Walnut Grove, California: AltaMira, 2006).

9   J. L. Moreno and Zerka Toeman, "The Group Approach in Psychodrama," *Sociometry*, 1942, 5(2): 191–195; J. L. Moreno, "Psychodrama and Group Psychotherapy," *Sociometry*, 1946, 9(2/3): 249–253.

1

Exploring Possibilities (*Runes of Magic*)

Abstract: *The challenges and opportunities associated with role-playing deceased persons inside virtual worlds are so many and diverse that this initial chapter aims to introduce their typical features rather than extreme variations as in some later chapters. It is a reconnaissance of a technically fine but somewhat bland virtual world,* Runes of Magic, *using an avatar based on a deceased person about whom we have at present only limited information. As the word* avatar *was adapted from Hindu religion by computer programmers years ago to describe the virtual reflection of the user, we suggest adapting the Hindu-Buddhist term* sattva *to name the purified essence of a person, which defines the character of an avatar. Surviving unpublished writings by the person represented in this chapter define his literary orientation toward fantasy and death, and the mythos of* Runes of Magic *considers its virtual world to be an evolved form of a book. The chapter shows the series of steps a user must go through to create an avatar and develop it through the early levels of experience inside the typical gameworld, including a variety of activities subsidiary to the main theme of adventures gained exploring an exotic world.*

Bainbridge, William Sims. *An Information Technology Surrogate for Religion : The Veneration of Deceased Family in Online Games.* New York: Palgrave MacMillan, 2014.
DOI: 10.1057/9781137490599.0003.

> Sattva: The purified essence of a person, which defines the character of an avatar.

The challenges and opportunities associated with role-playing deceased persons inside virtual worlds are so many and diverse that an initial reconnaissance should avoid unnecessary subtleties. Therefore our first memorial avatar will be based on an interesting but rather remote individual, Ernest E. Wheeler (1876–1955), inside a technically fine but somewhat bland virtual world, *Runes of Magic*. Ernest was not only a Harvard-educated New York attorney, but also a cantankerous joker, who used to debate the minister in church during sermons, and who transformed the real historical murder of his father's best friend into a story of mythic proportions. The special wiki devoted to *Runes* describes its virtual world: "Taborea was once a book in which the creation of a simple world of flora and fauna was supposed to be recorded, but today it is full of myths and legends. The continents are covered by baffling and cryptic traces of time long gone. In the Age of discovery the people of Taborea are now on a quest to find out about their mystical past."[1]

Ancestor veneration

Across the millennia, humans have practiced a wide range of rituals to manage the existential problem of death. That diversity reflects the fact that we have as yet found no perfect solution, but it also results from the fact that death is a swarm of problems. When a member of one's family dies, one may feel guilty that one did not do enough to save that life. One may still have unpaid debts to that person, even just in the form of thanks for the help they offered during the survivors' childhoods. The people close to us serve as mentors, and we may wish the lessons to continue after the demise of the teacher. Survivors need to manage their relations with each other, in the shared dislocation caused by the loss of a member of the group. The death of someone near to us implies that death is approaching us as well. One of the classical theories of the origin of religion is that it consolidated from the consolations people shared at the deaths of loved ones, initially in the form of rituals of ancestor veneration.[2]

The term "AVA" describes an avatar based on a deceased person. Originally, this is the acronym from *Ancestor Veneration Avatar*.[3] Ernest

DOI: 10.1057/9781137490599.0003

had no children, so technically he was not the ancestor of anyone. However, he was part of the ancestral family of myself, my cousins, and of our children. AVA can also mean *Avatar for Virtual Awakening*, in which we ourselves awaken to new possibilities of consciousness, even as we reawaken a lost soul. *Avatar*, of course, is a religious term from Hinduism that refers to the terrestrial manifestation of some aspect of a deity, but has been adopted for characters in virtual worlds that significantly embody the personal identity of the user.

An AVA does represent the user to some extent, but also represents another person, whom I call the *sattva*. This term comes from the same cultural tradition as *avatar*, and I am not really misusing *sattva* but reinterpreting it, as was done with *avatar* decades ago. The Buddhist term *bodhisattva* refers to purified saints who are unusually enlightened and from whom we can learn transcendent truths. In using *sattva* for the being represented by an AVA, I stress that it is a *purified form* of the real deceased person, using the memories and other information we have about that person to construct a virtual spiritual guide that will lead us through a series of enlightening adventures. In the case of Ernest E. Wheeler, however, I did not know him very well, so part of the challenge is discovering him.

The importance of being Ernest

When preparing to create an avatar based on a deceased person one did not know very well, one should catalog all the memories one has about the person, and then augment them with whatever other information might be available. In the case of Ernest, I seem to have exactly one clear memory. I was a small boy, visiting my grandparents' house at Maple Hill Farm, a short walk up the road from our own dwelling, in Bethel, Connecticut. Ernest was the brother of my grandmother, and I recall that he was a lean gentleman with a New England accent. He is sitting on the front porch and asks me to sit on his knee. He bounces me up and down, then pretends to drop me on the floor, but catches me at the last moment.

I also recall a few things that members of the family told me about Ernest, and one of those second-hand memories is so vivid it may be a mixture of what I was told and what I saw. We lived in a small house that had rather low ceilings. When Ernest visited, he would often act out

DOI: 10.1057/9781137490599.0003

the same humorous ritual. He would step from our living room into the library, slap his hand on the top of the door frame and shout, "Oh my head!" Perhaps the first time, our family thought he had really cracked his skull, but soon they realized he had cracked a joke. Ernest was a life-long bachelor, and within the family it was said that this resulted from disappointment in a failed romance he experienced early in life, about which I have been able to learn nothing.

When preparing virtual revival for a deceased person, one step is to write down any memories one recalls, and add others as they come to mind. A second step is to assemble any documents one possesses. A third step is to request information from other members of the family. In the case of Ernest, my son Lars Bainbridge possessed a file of papers that he first described by long-distance telephone, then scanned some into his computer and sent them via email. Lars also reported the result of online searches he had done years before, finding that Ernest had been centrally involved in a 1934–1935 case that reached the US Supreme Court, Shanferoke Coal and Supply Corporation versus Westchester Service Corporation, which involved a dispute about an agreement to purchase large amounts of coal over a period of years.

The documents included a death notice, which was sent to newspa-pers, and printed in condensed form by at least one.[4] With respect to his character, it described him as "a polemicist, writing extensively on many controversial matters of the day." Some of those matters were crucially important, and he took positions that would be respected today, such as when he left the Republican Party because it rejected American membership in the League of Nations, and was among the leadership of the American League of Nations Association. Some of the matters may seem trivial, but one of those connects him to the fantasy and horror ethos of many MMOs.

On an advertisement for a performance of the play, *The Scarecrow* by Percy MacKaye, he had scrawled "They never hear of Hawthorne's Feathertop!" Indeed, as MacKaye acknowledged in a preface to the published script, it was inspired by, if not exactly adapted from, "Feathertop: A Moralized Legend" by Nathaniel Hawthorne.[5] This was a short story about a New England witch who brings a well-dressed scare-crow to life, and sends it into the world of fashion and commerce, since most real men there also totally lack substance.[6] Ernest corresponded directly with MacKaye, and with drama critic Walter Prichard Eaton,

DOI: 10.1057/9781137490599.0003

who both had been at Harvard when Ernest was there, asserting that Hawthorne's work was superior to MacKaye's and deserved more respect. At one point, Ernest commented, "The trouble with the theater is that it is too often theatrical." But notice that MMO role-playing is a kind of very theatrical theater, in which a member of the audience takes center-stage, just as Ernest attempted to do in this agitated correspondence. Hawthorne called the scarecrow a *simulacrum* rather than an *avatar*, yet it functioned as the avatar of the witch.

Ernest's death notice also recognized that he had served in the First World War, ending with the rank of major, but perhaps not seeing action: "His Army posts included that of Inspector of the National Army Training Detachment at colleges under the War Department committee on Education and Special Training." It also reported: "He was an enthusiastic canoeist and woodsman, having paddled down many rivers in Canada, along the Eastern seaboard of the United States, in England, and down the Moldau in ancient Bohemia." Thus, it was unclear whether an authentic AVA of him would enjoy virtual combat, but it would certainly enjoy exploration of informatic wilderness.

In preparation for creating an AVA, one has the choice to delve deeply into the context of the person's life through online sources, or not, depending upon the goals of the exercise. Two real estate websites let me see a picture of the apartment building where Ernest died, learn it was built in 1929, and read: "This prewar Upper East Side Art Deco building features old world charm and elegance." Of course one may visit any real-world site important in the life of a sattva, and as of June 13, 2014, I could have rented a one-bedroom apartment in the building for $3,500 per month. My most influential information about Ernest came, however, from a photocopy of memories of family history he dictated a few months before his death, which I had puzzled over for decades.

I was told that this remarkable document was not entirely accurate. For example, Ernest wrote about the adventures his father had when he went west from his native Maine to California during the gold rush. According to family legend, Thomas Heber Wheeler (1838–1908) wanted to marry Ellen Elizabeth Hyde (1843–1933), but they were mere children and her father would not consider the proposition until Thomas had proven his ability to support her in prosperity. One of the adventures, as Ernest described it, could well have been a quest arc in a massively multiplayer online game:

DOI: 10.1057/9781137490599.0003

My father had on the left side of his head a wound in the scalp, which we children could feel and then listen to the account of its infliction. It seems that one early evening his elderly partner was on the shore of a stream washing or panning out gold, and in so doing assumed a crouching position. My father was at the camp higher up the bank and was cooking their evening supper consisting of corn beef hash. When it was ready he stepped onto the bank to call his partner and was horrified to see a desperado, an "enemy" of the old man, creeping up behind him with a long knife. Thomas was too late, for the desperado plunged it into the old man's abdomen, and as my father described, giving force by effective gestures, "twisted it about." This twisting and turning of the knife was the very acme of our horror, and in my boyish re-narration I found it extremely effective, particularly if I suddenly used one of my audience as a subject to try it on.

My father says of his old partner, "He died in my arms." Even now that scene of these two, the boy and the man, the boy with his arms around the old man, is, to me, touching in the extreme. I used to wait for Father to say, "He died in my arms." They were on the outskirts of a mining settlement, which became later a county seat. Father aroused the miners and there was a high sheriff, none other than Jim Stetson, whose sister later married Charles Wheeler. The high sheriff at once swore in a posse and Father presented himself to Jim, who said, "This is a boy. He has no beard," as he stroked Father's chin. The miners intervened on Father's behalf, and he was accepted by Jim. One of the mounted bands by good luck captured the murderer within upwards of twenty-four hours, and he was held by the sheriff in a makeshift jail, which was merely a log cabin.

A rumor spread that a band of desperadoes had organized to rescue the murderer. This story my father believed, and with good reason. He succeeded in organizing a lynching party. Father later came to see that the miners probably thought Stetson would only make a show of resistance, and would indeed be glad to get rid of his "guest" in so simple and effective a manner. It turned out they were wrong. Though Stetson warned the party that he would protect his prisoner by force of arms, they manned a long log, four on a side, with the boy at the front where he insisted on placing himself, and on the run, plunged it against the jail door. As the door crashed, Father was first to be shoved in directly in front of Stetson. Stetson did indeed resort to force of arms. He brought the butt of his pistol down on Father's head, knocking him out completely. This accounts for the scar, and my fingers still tingle as I tell about it. After my father's knockout by the sheriff, the would-be lynchers fell back, knowing that the sheriff meant what he said. The murderer was finally hanged after due process of the law.

DOI: 10.1057/9781137490599.0003

The vivid manner in which Ernest wrote suggests that this episode had acquired a legendary quality, and both he and his father before him may have exaggerated details for dramatic effect. It says much about Ernest's love for his father, but also reveals Ernest's own role in life. The last word in the anecdote is "law," and the lynch mob sought to take law into its own hands. As a professional lawyer, Ernest may often have felt tension in his work, because the actual labor is meticulous, but the cases often concern frantic conflict. In preparation for writing this chapter, I decided to see if I could learn anything more about the incident by searching online.

First of all, Wikipedia has a page for Charles Stetson Wheeler, the son of the Charles Wheeler mentioned in the story, and Angeline Stetson. Their wedding took place in "the gold rush town of Columbia, California, on April 17, 1859."[7] A somewhat obscure website called Ripple posts historical "nuggets" about the history of gold prospecting, including a reminiscence written in 1922 by Charles R. Stetson that calls "Mr. Wheeler" "my brother-in-law" and identifies Angeline as his sister, so clearly he was talking about Charles Wheeler. The Stetson family was living in Massachusetts when the gold rush began, and he wrote, "In 1852 my oldest brother, James, who had just completed his trade of tinsmith caught the fever and joined our father in the mines." By 1855, James had become constable of Columbia, and Charles R. Stetson described the lynch mob very differently from the way Ernest did, writing as an eye witness, and not mentioning Ernest's father:

> The mob, however, was growing more noisy and exhibited a rope already prepared with the hangman's noose and well soaped. In the meantime, the Judge had committed the prisoner to the County Jail to await the action of the grand jury. The constable then cleared the little court room and prepared to take the prisoner to jail. The crowd outside had now become fully excited and began pressing in the doors having got one of them partially opened. My brother with pistol in hand ordered the crowd to stand back or he would shoot. The crowd fell back slightly and the door closed. There was a scantling 3x4 lying on the floor which had been left by workmen, I took it up and with the assistance of others braced the doors in such fashion that the only way to get through the doors was to cut them down. Soon an ax was procured and began to cut.[8]

Ernest did not give the name of his father's partner, but this account describes the killing as "the murder of Bond by McCauley." This information led me to a book by Herbert O. Lang about the history of the

DOI: 10.1057/9781137490599.0003

area, published in 1882 and thus much closer in time to the murder than Ernest's account. Bond had been a witness against McCauley in a larceny case, and the murder took place later during an argument in a saloon, not outdoors while panning for gold. Indeed, McCauley stabbed Bond in the left side with a bowie knife, but only after Bond had shot a friend of McCauley's named Carr.[9]

Everything about this murder scene is different from Ernest's account, except for the means by which Bond was killed, a knife to the gut. The general ambiance is the same however, and the gold rush days were as wild as many of the settings depicted in MMOs. Whatever the details, Thomas Heber Wheeler did return to Maine a rich man, married his childhood sweetheart, established a very successful shipping business, and had three children, each of whom relates to one of the first three chapters of this book.

Casting the Runes

On April 25, 2011, I created a character named Ernestwheeler in *Runes of Magic*, a reasonably popular fantasy MMO that has the unusual history of being created by a Taiwanese company, Runewaker Entertainment, and adapted for the Western market by a German one, Frogster Interactive. Character creation in MMOs takes place through a standard process in which the player has some superficial choices about how the character may appear, usually including the gender, and selects two functionally significant choices, *race* and *class*. The term *race* may seem offensive, yet it is the standard term for the nationality or ethnicity of the character, which often determines where in the virtual geography its life will begin, the lore and backstory that give meaning to its actions, and its location in the bloody factional conflict that dominates most MMOs.

Runes of Magic has three races: Humans, Dwarves, and Elves. Given my image of his character and appearance, clearly Ernestwheeler needed to be an Elf. The graphics are pleasant, if a bit cartoonish, and these qualities seem to fit Ernest well. The face of the Elf looked at least a little like the real man, and the huge pointed ears seemed to express his cantankerous nature. The game's wiki explains the lore: "The Elves have been mired in myth and war since time immemorial. These forces have sharpened the instincts of this ancient race, making them elegant hunters and masters in the art of battle."[10]

DOI: 10.1057/9781137490599.0003

Classes are distinct sets of abilities the character will possess, developing them over time but not radically changing them. Some recent MMOs are more flexible, allowing a character to gain skills more freely, but *Runes* was typical of older games in having rigid classes. Each race in this game had six classes, a different mix from a list of ten, and each class reflected modest variations built on a very traditional MMO division of labor. Often called the *trinity*, three basic roles are *tank* (heavily armored, able to battle toe-to-toe with the enemy), *DPS* (damage-per-second, often standing at a distance and hurling arrows or magic spells at the enemy), and *healer* (using magic to support the tank and DPS). The ten *Runes* classes combine elements of these roles in different ways, and with different symbolism. For example, both a scout and a mage are "ranged DPS" classes that damage the enemy from a distance, but scouts fire arrows while mages fire spells. Given the spiritual focus of this book, I was interested in four classes: (1) priest (healer, instrument of the divine), (2) mage (ranged DPS, master of the elements), (3) warlock (ranged DPS, exploiting the dark arts), and (4) druid (healer, commander of nature's might). Given that as an attorney, Ernest had sought to solve people's problems, and the priest class was not available for Elves, I decided he must be a druid.

Ernestwheeler entered the virtual world called Taborea in the Valley of Preparation, right near a pretty green-and-gold building in idealized ecclesiastical style called the Academy. MMOs typically begin in such a tutorial area, giving the player some very simple and rather safe missions that serve to teach the mechanics of the user interface and the general logic of action in the game. Other new players were also entering at the same place and time. Standing here and there were nonplayer characters (NPCs), some of which were marked with an exclamation mark over their heads, indicating that the player should interact with them. These NPCs tended to be what are called *quest givers*, offering a mission to the player. Often MMO missions merely ask the character to kill monsters or enemies, such as one Ernestwheeler accepted to exterminate five gluttonous snails that were polluting the Academy.

Traditional MMOs, but not a few of the newest ones, advance a character up a strict status ladder called *experience*. In combat, Ernestwheeler could reliably kill an enemy of the same level, easily vanquish lower ones, but would himself be vanquished by enemies a couple of levels above. Regions of the virtual world are distinguished by the typical level of enemies found in it, so ascending the experience ladder also means

DOI: 10.1057/9781137490599.0003

exploring new territories, and one cannot explore without ascending. He entered the Valley of Preparation at level 1, and departed at level 10. Early levels tend not only to be easy but to be completed swiftly, and progress slows down to the point that the top levels in some games may take as much as ten hours per level. For some later chapters, I took a character all the way to the maximum experience, called the *level cap*. That would have been around 75 for Runes, but I planned to memorialize Ernest only briefly, and set 25 as my goal.

From level 10 to 14, Ernestwheeler explored Elven Island, the wider Elf starting zone that included the Valley of Preparation. Then he left his race's home island by way of the Haven of Departure and traveled to the multi-racial city that would be his home base, Varanas. Many MMOs possess virtual cities, sometimes several of them devoted either to a race, a faction composed of several allied races, or a particular range of experience levels.

The Central Plaza in Varanas had a bank on one side and an auction house on the other, two facilities common in high-quality MMOs. A character typically carries several bags that can hold all kinds of virtual things, including goods looted from deceased enemies and magic potions for healing one's own wounds. But their capacity is limited, so a vault in the bank can be used to store valuable things that might be used later. Each MMOs has a complex economy, and many possess an online market through which players may buy and sell things with each other, here in the form of an auction house. The southern section of the city was called Administration, and had a hall for members of the ten classes, plus one for guilds, virtual organizations to which players could belong. The northern section, or Lower City, houses a large number of businesses where NPC vendors sell goods and to which an avatar could sell loot, as well as crafting stations where avatars can create goods from raw materials collected outside, and NPC quest givers.

Questing for meaning

From this point onward, Ernestwheeler would venture outside the city into zones of countryside appropriate for his experience level, carry out missions for NPC quest givers located there, and return to Varanas occasionally to conduct business. Although druids have the right skills to support teammates in combat, he primarily did solo-player missions, although he did join a player-created guild named Exodus. Many of the formal missions involved sacred archaeology, such as copying inscriptions from ancient stone tablets, and investigating mysterious altars guarded by spirits. Yet, in general, his tasks and explorations required killing vast numbers of NPC monsters and enemies. In the basement of Forsaken Abbey, he exterminated filthy carrion spiders and rat-ear bats, while also collecting ancient documents. Bandit Kobolds had stolen the research notes for a history project, "Legends of Taborea," so Ernestwheeler battled them repeatedly to collect all the lost pages, including the crucial thirteenth:

> The highest god wrote a book
> Its name was Taborea
> Creating the land we mortals live
> The eternal Taborea
> Beautiful poems formed the sky and the seas
> Profound words the trees and the mountains
> Blessing the glory of life

One of the more interesting *Runes of Magic* quest arcs came to its climax in the home of Hugo the hermit on an island in the Lake of Magic Mist, and deals directly with supernatural dimensions of death and immortality. Ernestwheeler had been sent there by Musa, another hermit, to combat the evil witch Ancalon, who has possessed Forsaken Abbey. She is no ordinary evil witch, but a well-meaning person who bound evil into her body to protect others from it, and thus is the victim of self-sacrifice. While she controls the Abbey, she is also a prisoner in it. This is a metaphor about life, because death is the only real escape, yet death seems a total loss of freedom.

In order to accept absolute evil into her body, Ancalon had to dispose of her soul, which she formed into a pearl. Now Hugo told Ernestwheeler to take her old hair ornament from a box and use it to release her soul from the pearl. This caused Ancalon to appear and do battle with Ernestwheeler, who summoned a magical Spirit of the Oak to assist him. Once defeated, she returns to her old, good self, and speaks to Hugo before vanishing into nonexistence:

> I have something very important to tell you. My soul has no strength left for those demons to feed upon, so they are seeking a new source to replace me ... and that would free them from the bonds of their seal ... you must stop them.

DOI: 10.1057/9781137490599.0003

Do you still remember that box that I valued so highly? Within it lies a gift that I left for you and Lythin for the Saint's Blessing Festival ... I hope these gifts can somehow take my place on your journey.

Remember that I love you, and please give Lythin my love. Goodbye, my dear Hugo...

Hugo shouts a futile protest as Ancalon disappears. He, as it happens, was her husband, and Lythin was their daughter. When Ancalon became a witch, Hugo placed Lythin in the care of Musa to separate her from the evil, so this story refers to a calamity experienced by a family, which separated them from each other even before death. Thinking about this tragedy, I naturally wondered why the real Ernest Wheeler had been something of a hermit, and contemplated how all humans are gravely affected by the struggles of the people close to them.

In 2014, I briefly revisited *Runes of Magic*, not to take Ernestwheeler above level 25 of general experience, but to gain experience with the three gathering skills through which resources can be harvested from the environment, reaching level 20 in both woodcutting and herbalism, and level 24 in mining. During missions, his avatar had looted many valuable things, including two yellow rings that required having achieved experience level 20. But I remembered that I had inherited a ring from my father that he in turn had inherited from the original Ernest Wheeler. So, I sent Ernestwheeler to the Varanas auction house, to see what he could buy that was fancy but affordable with the 135,000 gold coins he then possessed. A player's avatar named Zamantha was selling for 75,000 gold coins a fjord ring that would magically increase the owner's stamina, health, dexterity, and defense, so Ernestwheeler bought it, despite his awareness that it could not be worn before reaching level 85 of general experience, something he would never achieve.

The fact that it was possible to revive Ernestwheeler after three years illustrates the fact that many virtual worlds are persistent, providing a degree of information longevity for avatars. The fact that I could not take his fjord ring out of *Runes*, illustrates the limitations of inheritance across different modes of reality. Yet inheritance is meaningful for humans. After Ernest Wheeler's death in 1955, his sister June received a letter from her elder son, saying: "I particularly wanted something really personal of Uncle's, and am so pleased that I got his ring. You know the one I mean—the one which he was very proud of and had received, I believe, from a grateful client. It was all very amusing. Of course, everything was listed at a very, very low price for tax purposes. You may recall the ring

DOI: 10.1057/9781137490599.0003

was listed as a cat's eye stone and appraised at $15.00. I took the ring the next day to a very reputable jeweler to have it made larger, only to find that the stone is a star sapphire and worth a good deal."[11] The sapphire does contain a star and is set in gold that is shaped like a panther battling a dragon, and thus a good symbol for the fantasies humans invest in the creations of their technology.

Conclusion

Social interaction requires humans to develop in their minds cognitive models of the minds of other people. Thus, even before the invention of theater, people could "take the role of the other."[12] When a loved-one dies, the neurological equivalent of a simulation of that person lives on in the minds of the survivors. Thus, an AVA is a computer simulation that serves to expand a neurological simulation, in pursuit of meaning that might be called spiritual. In running an AVA through an MMO, we can exercise many of our mental and emotional faculties, understanding the complex environment in terms that would have been meaningful to the sattva. When Ernest told exaggerated stories about his father's adventures in the Gold Rush, he was performing a pre-computational virtual revival. All virtual worlds are based on laws, although programmed into the software rather than codified through legislation that must be acted upon by humans. Thus it seemed fitting to experience Ernest as an Elf who undertook mission for quest givers, just as an attorney takes cases from clients.

Notes

1   runesofmagic.gamepedia.com/Taborea.
2   Meyer Fortes, "Pietas in Ancestor Worship." *Journal of the Royal Anthropological Institute of Great Britain and Ireland*, 1961, 91(2): 166–191.
3   William Sims Bainbridge, "Ancestor Veneration Avatars," in *Handbook of Research on Technoself: Identity in a Technological Society*, edited by Rocci Luppicini (Hershey, Pennsylvania: Information Science Reference, 2013), pp. 308–321; "Perspectives on Virtual Veneration," *The Information Society*, 2013, 29: 196–212.
4   "Ernest E. Wheeler: Lived Here 30 Years," *Herald Statesman*, Yonkers, New York, February 23, 1955, p. 2.

DOI: 10.1057/9781137490599.0003

5   Percy MacKaye, *The Scarecrow or the Glass of Truth: A Tragedy of the Ludicrous* (New York: Macmillan, 1911).

6   Nathaniel Hawthorne, *Mosses from an Old Manse* (Boston: Houghton, Mifflin, 1883), pp. 253–278.

7   en.wikipedia.org/wiki/Charles_Stetson_Wheeler.

8   minerdiggins.com/Ripple/gville/gv002a.html.

9   Herbert O. Lang, *A History of Tuolumne County, California* (San Francisco: B. F. Alley, 1882), pp. 216–217.

10 runesofmagic.gamepedia.com/Elf.

11 Letter from William Wheeler Bainbridge to June Wheeler Bainbridge, April 27, 1955.

12 George Herbert Mead, *Mind, Self and Society from the Standpoint of a Social Behaviorist* (Chicago, Illinois: University of Chicago Press, 1934).

DOI: 10.1057/9781137490599.0003

2
Selecting a World (*Uru: Myst Online*)

Abstract: *The chapter considers the goal of* consonance, *achieving a functional harmony between a person and a virtual world that makes it a suitable environment for an avatar based on that person. Most computer games in which the user assumes a virtual identity are violent, but the person revived here was a very nonviolent woman, so there was a challenge finding a suitable home for her. First, she entered a relatively popular and quite spiritual online role-playing game,* Aion, *then discovered half way through its levels of experience that she would be forced to become unacceptably violent if she continued. Therefore, she took the advice of a leading female researcher on virtual gameworlds to shift to one based on puzzle-solving rather than combat, called* Myst, *thus illustrating one of the boundaries of the genre, and showing how a gameworld need not be popular to serve quasi-religious purposes. To provide a broad overview of the possibilities, she explored* Myst *in three very different forms, briefly the original solo-player computer game, more extensively the unpopular Internet-based social sequel,* Uru: Myst Online, *and very briefly the active* Myst *community in the nongame virtual world,* Second Life.

Bainbridge, William Sims. *An Information Technology Surrogate for Religion: The Veneration of Deceased Family in Online Games.* New York: Palgrave MacMillan, 2014.
DOI: 10.1057/9781137490599.0004.

> Consonance: A functional harmony between a person and a virtual
> world that makes it a suitable environment for an avatar based on
> that person.

Most computer games in which the user assumes a virtual identity are
violent, but Ernest's sister and my grandmother, June Ellen Wheeler
Bainbridge (1879–1967), was an exceedingly nonviolent person.
Therefore, this chapter demonstrates how a little effort can allow the
user to find a virtual environment in which the avatar would feel at
home. First, June will enter a relatively popular and quite spiritual online
role-playing game, *Aion*, then discover half way through its levels of
experience that she would be forced to become unacceptably violent if
she continued. Therefore, she took the advice of a leading researcher on
virtual gameworlds to shift to one based on puzzle-solving rather than
combat, called *Myst*, thus illustrating one of the boundaries of the genre,
and showing how a gameworld need not be popular to serve quasi-
religious purposes. To provide for this chapter a broad overview of the
possibilities, she explored *Myst* in three very different forms, the original
solo-player computer game, the Internet-based social sequel, *Uru: Myst
Online*, and very briefly the active Myst community in the nongame
virtual world, *Second Life*.

Ascent of an angel

Born on the first of June 1879, she was given the name of her birth
month, and the natural optimism and sunny disposition that it symbolized. June's daughter, Barbara Bainbridge McIntosh, reported: "My
mother valued sweetness, light, modesty, and good reputation. One of
her favorite Bible verses said, 'Let not then your good be evil spoken of'
(Romans 14:16). In other words, don't do anything that you may think
right in a way that could be misinterpreted. Another was: 'Whatsoever
things are lovely, whatsoever things are of good report ... think on these
things' (Philippians 4:8). And: 'Let the words of my mouth, and the
meditation of my heart, be acceptable in thy sight, O LORD, my strength,
and my redeemer' (Psalms 19:14). 'I will lift up mine eyes unto the hills,
from whence cometh my help' (Psalms 121:1). She wanted her children
to 'rejoice' and to feel safe in the goodness that has been transmitted to
us: 'He shall cover thee with his feathers, and under his wings shalt thou

DOI: 10.1057/9781137490599.0004

trust' (Psalms 91:4). But too, she wanted us strong and steadfast in afflic-
tion like Job."

Sweetness, light, and nonviolence do not imply laziness. Before her
marriage, her life was filled with visits by members of her extended
family, trips to Boston or Maine, evenings at the theater, French lessons,
Sunday School teaching, and constant attention from a number of
men who seemed to think that being her husband would be a fine fate.
She played bridge whist and ping pong. She read Heine, Browning,
Shakespeare, and Kipling aloud to her devoted younger brother Ernest.
She served in the Women's Benevolent Society, the executive committee
of The Neighborhood Home, and the alumnae association for the Veltin
School. She loved writing poetry, drawing, and painting watercolors of
outdoor scenes. After her 1911 marriage to William Seaman Bainbridge,
each year their Christmas card was a drawing with a verse, both by her.
Despite having vast documentation and many memories of her life,
I searched Internet, finding to our family's surprise yet another verse,
which served as the preface to a book published by the Maine Federation
of Women's Clubs in 1916, and was intended to be sung to the tune of the
national hymn, "America:"

> My father's state, to thee,
> First state of all to me,
> My love I bring.
> In they sweet woods I'll roam,
> Thy name to me is home,
> Pine trees and ocean foam,
> Thy praise I sing.[1]

Bridge whist and ping pong are games, but other artforms share some
qualities with computer games, music prominent among them. June
did not compose, but she played piano. Both piano and computer
are keyboard instruments, and a musical composition is a kind of
program. As in playing many computer games, one must do what the
composer intended, but in one's own style. June's daughter quoted her
and commented: "'Even some great concert pianists can't play hymns
properly. You have to have a feel for it, keeping the tune uppermost with
the right hand, slightly emphasizing the top note.' She played the hymns
for her Sunday School and sometimes for her Church and for the family
she grew up in and the family she made. The chords were all there in
both hands, but there were no pyrotechnics. The melody notes rode the
rich chords beneath."

DOI: 10.1057/9781137490599.0004

She traveled extensively, and her second grand tour of Europe in 1907 was especially intense. She was informally attached to a fact-finding junket of the United States Commission on Immigration headed by Republican Senator William Paul Dillingham of Vermont.[2] Her cousin William R. Wheeler, later to be assistant secretary of commerce and labor, was Theodore Roosevelt's appointee, and the party was rounded out by Senator Latimer, 3 congressmen, and 16 assorted friends and relations. Cousin "Billy" brought his wife Alice, and June shared a cabin with Olive Latimer, "a frivolous, kindhearted, very southern girl of twenty."[3] The aim of the trip was to learn the emigration policies of various nations, thus to help the United States decide its immigration policy. The six official members of the commission would split into three pairs. One would investigate the situation in Greece, Asia Minor, and Turkey, while another would do the same in Germany, Belgium, Holland, and France. Wheeler and Dillingham would deal with Austria-Hungary and Russia.[4] The ladies—called "appendices" by a Washington newspaper[5]—would travel around with the others, adding beauty to the voyage. June rode a gondola through the canals of Venice with Dillingham.[6] They took walks in Vienna, Budapest, St. Petersburg, Berlin, Paris, and London. In St. Petersburg, they marveled at the beauty of St. Isaac's church, with its ten columns of malachite and two of lapis lazuli.

From real to virtual

So, the ideal virtual world for the avatar I would call *Junellen* need not be limited to the Maine woods, but should also include places of great elegance. Although released by the major Korean game company, NCSoft, *Aion* was intended for a world audience, so its culture was highly cosmopolitan. Yet it was also very coherent, based on a well-developed mythos that could well be described as religious. Its Wikipedia article explains the origins of the world June entered in June 2011:

> When the god Aion created the world of Atreia, They [sic] created the Drakan—powerful dragon-like beasts tasked with safeguarding the humans; performing Aion's will on the planet; and protecting the Tower of Eternity, Aion's physical presence on Atreia. For a time, the Drakan obeyed Aion; but over time, they began to enjoy their power, ignoring their duties and abusing the humans who inhabited Atreia. Aion took notice, creating the twelve Empyrean Lords in response. Angelic in appearance, the Empyrean Lords were

DOI: 10.1057/9781137490599.0004

demigods who walked amongst humans, and used a force called "Aether" to create a powerful barrier, later to be called an aetheric field, around the Tower of Eternity, protecting all of those within. While the outside world continued to be ravaged by the Drakan, who had become the more ferocious Balaur; the humans within the barrier managed to tap into the Aether, gaining their own powers. In time, they would become known as the Daeva.[7]

So, Aion is a god, and the Daeva are humans "who have achieved ascension through hardships or a twist of fate which awakens their potential to become Demi-Gods."[8] But there were two factions of Daeva, the apparently angelic Elyos, to which June naturally belonged, and the apparently infernal Asmodians. *Elyon* is an ancient Hebrew word sometimes used to refer to God most High, while in Talmudic legends, Asmodeus was a king of demons.[9] The designers' intent was to employ symbols that might broadly appeal across many world cultures. It should also be remembered that Korea was the Asian nation in which Christianity became most popular. It happens that one of the factors accomplishing this was the Nevius Plan, developed by John Nevius, a member of the extended family June married into, who stressed local autonomy for missionaries and incidentally wrote a book about Asian beliefs in spirit possession.[10]

As in *Runes of Magic*, a player begins *Aion* by selecting a class that is a line of skill specialization associated with a set of symbols. Given the wider Aion mythos, for research purposes this needed to be a supernaturally oriented class, but the priest class seemed too conventional and would require working in teams of players and healing their warriors in combat, so I chose mage class for Junellen. The selection screen in the game described it thus: "Mages delight in dealing awe-inspiring levels of damage, but they are physically weak so they must be clever to survive. When they ascend, Mages become Sorcerers (with direct magical attacks) or Spiritmasters (who command powerful elemental spirits)." June did not like dealing damage, but words like "delight" harmonized with her spirit. In a fantasy, she was quite prepared to go some distance outside her gentle nature, as I recall a time she led my sister and me in an Ouija board communication with the spirit of a deceased ancient Babylonian.

The early territory and missions of an MMO, and of many solo-player games as well, form a tutorial. Junellen accepted many somewhat bland missions from NPCs, that gave me practice with the user interface, and gave her instruction in the contingencies of life in Atreia. A mage trainer would periodically teach her new abilities. If she came near death in a battle, she would be whisked to a sacred obelisk to which he had earlier

DOI: 10.1057/9781137490599.0004

bound her soul, but her soul would be damaged and require magi-cal repair. To the extent that she could, Junellen accepted nonviolent missions in preference over violent ones, but for a while even the latter were rather innocent in style.

At level 9 up *Aion's* ladder of experience, she began the process of *ascension*, which among other things gave her wings with which to fly, and at level 10 she reached the Elyos city called *Sanctum* that floats high in the sky. It reminded Junellen of Venice, a city June loved, but with streams of wind rather than water running through the streets. In 1938, she had written a poem about Venice, including this stanza:

> When boats are like a raven's wing
> And the boatman sings at his oar
> I know it's not an earthly thing
> But a bit of fairy lore.

Unfortunately, 1938 was followed by 1939 and the Second World War. When Junellen reached level 25 in Aion, she was forced to face the grim fact that any future progress would require her to engage in player-versus-player combat, directly seeking to kill the characters belonging to the Asmodian faction, something she refused to do. Given her familiar-ity with Europe, augmented by several trips there in the period between the two world wars, June had the perspective to understand the Second World War. Early in the period of US involvement, she accompanied her husband on a tour of Latin America, where he met with leaders of the various nations' military medical commands, as part of a broadly based effort to convince them to avoid an alliance with Germany, and perhaps to ally themselves with the United States. As her obituary in the *New York Times* noted, she was active in Bundles for Britain, a women's organiza-tion that donated clothing and medical supplies to the British, beginning in 1940.[11] In 1945, when the conflict came to its bloody close, she wrote the following poem:

> This is the time of bitterness
> When the mighty fall,
> When each man thinks he knows the right
> And blames another for it all.

> Surging waves of hate and greed
> Roll up and crash upon the shore
> And eddy round the swirling sand
> And steal up to your door.

DOI: 10.1057/9781137490599.0004

No man is safe within his wall
And dread stalks through the night.
"Where will the next blow fall," he cries,
"When goes my loved one from my sight?"

Yet soft and sweet steals back the day
And meadows gleam with dew,
And still the sun rides high at noon
And gardens bloom anew.

Through all the chaos runs a stream
And keeps its steady course.
We cannot reckon whence it came
Nor understand its force.

But there it flows, and though the wrecks
Float on its shiny wave,
It shall restore a stricken world
For the steadfast and the brave.

The title, "Out of the Depths," is the first line of Psalm 130: "Out of the depths have I cried unto thee, O Lord." While June would never claim to be a great poet, these verses are logically constructed and express a clear even forceful perspective on conflict. She reveals herself to be a realist as well as an idealist, who fully understands the meaning of evil. Among her greatest sorrows was the death of her first child, a daughter born with a fatal defect, but her joys were the three children she raised to adulthood. Near the very end of her life, she suffered from Alzheimer's, and lost many of her memories while preserving intact her gentle personality, a fate her younger son, John, recapitulated exactly. When June's elder son, William, was accidentally killed in 1965, her daughter, Barbara McIntosh, thought it best not to tell her mother, lest the shock be too much. Thus, letters the deceased son had written were re-read to her as if they were new, and June never recognized this benevolent subterfuge, thinking her son still lived.

An island in the mists

While Junellen could not continue in Aion, her spirit deserved further metaphoric revival. Where? I sought advice, having in mind how June herself might have done it. She had been a very active member of the feminist cultural organization, Sorosis, even serving as its president in

DOI: 10.1057/9781137490599.0004

1935–1939, so logically she would have sought the advice of a woman of the kind who belonged to Sorosis. She would have been interested to meet my colleague at the National Science Foundation, Rosanna Guadagno, and read her essays on how men and women differ in their orientations toward virtual worlds.[12] But what we really needed was an expert who would recommend the ideal game.

I am sure that June would have liked Celia Pearce, a game designer, teacher, and co-founder of a women's game collective. One of Pearce's observational research projects was an exploration of an unusual MMO she said was comfortable for women called *Uru: Ages Beyond Myst*, featured in a book Pearce co-authored with her avatar, Artemesia, called *Communities of Play*.[13] Unfortunately, *Uru* had never become commercially viable and had gone through a series of beta tests and closures.

This MMO was "beyond Myst," because it was one of several sequels to an exceedingly artistic and influential 1993 solo-player computer game called *Myst*. I had been aware of its fame at the time, and played the sequel, *Riven*, when it came out in 1997. I myself found *Riven* rather boring, with slow movements, mostly static environments, and too many obscure puzzles to solve. In retrospect, I thought June might have liked these gentle games. The Wikipedia article for *Myst* describes the general pattern for the entire series:

> *Myst* puts the player in the role of the Stranger, who uses a special book to travel to the island of Myst. There, the player uses other special books written by an artisan and explorer named Atrus to travel to several worlds known as "Ages." Clues found in each of these Ages help to reveal the back-story of the game's characters. The game has several endings, depending on the course of action the player takes. Upon release, *Myst* was a surprise hit, with critics lauding the ability of the game to immerse players in the fictional world. The game was the best-selling PC game, until *The Sims* exceeded its sales in 2002. *Myst* helped drive adoption of the then-nascent CD-ROM format. *Myst's* success spawned four direct video game sequels as well as several spin-off games and novels.[14]

Twenty years after its release, I tried *Myst*, imagining that June was the Stranger, although the game is experienced in a first-person view, seeing through the eyes of the avatar, rather than looking down on the avatar from above and behind as in most MMOs. I imagined that she would have found it more interesting than I did, and only went so far as to solve the puzzles required to leave the island. Designed for the rather limited

DOI: 10.1057/9781137490599.0004

computers of 20 years ago, *Myst* displays a sequence of static pictures and does not depict the user as an avatar. Except for a few small-scale animations, there is little movement, and the challenge for the user is to select the right choice among a small number of alternatives.

Eight switches are found here and there on the island. They must be counted and seven of them put in the up position. In a library, four books can be opened and read, each one being the diary of an explorer who visited a quartet of strange "ages" that the player might later explore: Channelwood, Mechanical, Stoneship, and Spaceship. The first book describes Channelwood: "Water covers this age as far as I can see except for a small rocky island. Elsewhere, there are only trees, which grow directly out of the water. A myriad of thin wooden passageways are built just above the water and disappear into the forest." After reading through this library, Junellen learned how to open a secret door behind the bookcase and found the codes necessary to open gateways to the four fantastic ages.

Solo-player games, whether designed for computers or videogame systems, vary greatly, and only some would be ideal for virtual revival. In many, one plays the role of a pre-defined character, whether an Italian plumber in all the Nintendo Mario games, or a fictional character such as Indiana Jones from the movies. Some do allow creation of a character with a name and some features selected by the player, as most MMOs do.

Seeking friends

From Celia Pearce, Junellen learned that a version of the MMO called *Myst Online: URU Live* existed at the moment, supported by donations and functioning outside the conventional market for games. She entered and found herself on a tiny island that belonged to her and her alone, but with a tiny house and a bookcase containing a couple of volumes that could transport her to other ages, where exploring and solving puzzles could earn her more books to build a library connecting to a complex virtual world. Each player had a personal island, which connected in groups to parallel copies of a neighborhood, and from each neighborhood one could begin to explore instances of the range of ages beyond those of the original *Myst*. The backstory is that an ancient civilization called the D'ni discovered or created the ages, then collapsed, so by

DOI: 10.1057/9781137490599.0004

carrying out the equivalent of virtual archaeology Junellen could gain access to the D'ni universe.

In theory, each of the many neighborhoods would be the center of vibrant social activity, but during Junellen's several visits in March through May 2013, there never seemed to be more than a dozen people inhabiting this virtual world at any given time, so her explorations were conducted solo and she attended only a few group meetings. However, her explorations were social in a very real sense, because she was constantly guided by a Wiki-like online database established by the Guild of Greeters, mostly dating from 2007: "The Guild of Greeters was established to assist new explorers to D'ni answering any questions they may have. Our mission is to ensure that a safe and fun time is had by all, and that someone will always be available to lend you a helping hand when you need it."[15] She never did interact in realtime with a Greeter, yet they always seemed present and helpful in her mind.

The first age she explored, a desert environment called Cleft, was effectively the tutorial for the other ages. There she encountered a nonplayer character named Zandi, sitting in the shade of a mobile home and reading a book. Indeed, books are the fundamental metaphor of *Myst*, and pages must be collected inside each age to achieve progress. Because of its somewhat primitive—or perhaps intentionally puzzling—interface, I found it difficult to take good pictures of Junellen in the environment, usually forced to look at the back of her head. The best portrait of her I got was when she was standing inside the fossilized jaw of a gigantic dragon in Cleft, touching and thus gaining one of these pages. When she finished all her many explorations, the bookcase held 17 books, and she felt quite satisfied she had experienced enough of what the ancient D'ni had to offer.

On several occasions she interacted socially with other players, but only in one session did she participate in a multiplayer puzzle mission, as a member of a team of ten that attempted the two most representative ones. They gathered in an age called Eder Delin, where there was a mysterious locked door on a cliff face. At various locations distant from the door were seven numbered cloths, the one nearest to the door being on the trunk of a tree. One member of the team needed to stand at each cloth as the leader called out numbers, 1 through 7, and quickly touch the cloth when its number was called. Only if all actions were performed correctly, would the door open. After succeeding at this, they repeated the process for a different mysterious door in the Eder Tsogal age. This

DOI: 10.1057/9781137490599.0004

all seemed very symbolic to Junellen, signifying cooperation in relation to mystery, hopefully gaining insight into the nature of existence through working together.

Knowing that there were *Myst* sims in *Second Life*, I created a Junellen avatar, and sent her to explore. The software's search tool allowed her to find both places and groups. She quickly joined the Myst/D'ni Community (153 members), Myst Online Explorers (417 members), and D'ni Refugees (730 members). Avatars in *Second Life* may belong to many groups, and unless a group expels inactive avatars the list will include many who were created by people years ago but who never log in today. Some may even be deceased. D'ni Refugees did seem to consist of active *Second Life* citizens, and when Junellen first joined fully 29 of them were online at the moment, and about 300 of them had been online in the past month. She visited two very nice ages, one imitating Channelwood and one called Eder Kiki, which included a seaside garden, an art gallery, and a castle. Inside the castle was a chapel where animation cushions allowed Junellen to kneel in prayer, and a virtual bible linked to the online resource BibleGateway. The last time I logged out from that avatar, I indeed left Junellen praying for continued existence, 46 years after her death. Perhaps the fundamental mystery of *Myst* concerns how much it is a metaphoric expression of Christian mysticism.

In a review of the original *Myst* game at ChristianAnswers.com, Carole Stewart McDonnell says it "is a story of family disharmony and betrayal (a subtle retelling of Cain and Abel and of a Fall). But who betrayed whom and why? To find out the mystery of this family saga, one has to get through all the 'ages' of the island. Clues are scattered all over in the form of symbols, electrical switches that go on and when flipped. Written notes and secret messages behind paintings, on pathways, behind secret doors."[16] She complains that insufficient guidance is offered to players, and therefore many will get lost. Of course, this is a standard issue for any religion, concerning how explicit it must be, which requires clear and authoritative leadership, versus requiring each supplicant to undertake individual spiritual exploration. Other commentators have also made the religious connection, asserting that the two brothers who created *Myst*, Rand and Robyn Miller, were Christians and thus were guided by their faith's values, whether or not specific features of the games were metaphors for specific biblical episodes or sacred principles.[17]

DOI: 10.1057/9781137490599.0004

Conclusion

Selecting an appropriate virtual world for the avatar of a given sattva is the most prominent example of emulation, acting as the living person would have done. We can never perfectly imitate the behavior of a deceased person, just as we cannot predict the exact behavior of a living one. But the attempt can be worthwhile, not merely as a form of pious veneration, but as an exploration of ways in which we may expand our own consciousness. To a significant extent, each of us is already the amalgam of the people we have known, and experiencing a virtual world through an AVA for many hours can clarify and magnify one of our many internal personalities. Perhaps most significantly, doing so from the vantage of a deceased person engages the deepest questions about the meaning of life.

Notes

1   June Wheeler Bainbridge, "Maine," preface to *The Trail of the Maine Pioneer* by Maine Federation of Women's Clubs (Lewiston, Maine: Lewiston Journal Company, 1916).

2   William Paul Dillingham, *Biographical Directory of the United States Congress 1774–1989* (Washington, DC: United States Government Printing Office, 1989), p. 911; " 'My Happiest Hour,' Told by Well-Known Men," *New York Times*, March 26, 1911, part 5, p. 10.

3   June Ellen Wheeler, letter to parents, May 20, 1907.

4   "Discourage Immigration," *New York Times*, August 13, 1907, p. 3.

5   June Ellen Wheeler, letter to parents, June 4, 1907.

6   June Ellen Wheeler, letter to parents, July 8, 1907.

7   en.wikipedia.org/wiki/Aion:_The_Tower_of_Eternity.

8   aion.wikia.com/wiki/Daeva.

9   en.wikipedia.org/wiki/Elyon, en.wikipedia.org/wiki/Asmodeus.

10   Helen S. Coan Nevius, *The Life of John Livingston Nevius* (New York: Fleming H. Revell, 1895); *Our Life in China* (New York: Robert Carter, 1869); John L. Nevius, *Demon Possession and Allied Themes, Being an Inductive Study of Phenomena of Our Own Times*, 3rd edn. (New York: Fleming H. Revell, 1896); en.wikipedia.org/wiki/John_Livingstone_Nevius.

11   Obituary: June Wheeler Bainbridge, *New York Times*, July 15, 1967.

12   Rosanna E. Guadagno, Nicole L. Muscanell, Bradley M. Okdie, Nanci M. Burk, and Thomas B. Ward, "Even in Virtual Environments Women Shop

DOI: 10.1057/9781137490599.0004

and Men Build: A Social Role Perspective on *Second Life.*" *Computers in Human Behavior*, 2011, 27: 304–308; Robert Andrew Dunn and Rosanna E. Guadagno, "My Avatar and Me—Gender and Personality Predictors of Avatar-Self Discrepancy." *Computers in Human Behavior*, 2012, 28: 97–106.

13 Celia Pearce and Artemesia, *Communities of Play* (Cambridge, MA: MIT Press, 2009).

14 en.wikipedia.org/wiki/Myst.

15 www.guildofgreeters.com/.

16 Carole Stewart McDonnell, "Myst," http://christiananswers.net/spotlight/games/2000/myst.html.

17 Erik Davis, "Into the Myst: The Miller Brothers' Virtual Tale," in *The Village Voice*, August 23, 1994, www.techgnosis.com/index_myst.html.

DOI: 10.1057/9781137490599.0004

3
Achieving a Goal (*Defiance*)

Abstract: *To provide contrast for the previous chapter that sought a nonviolent world, this chapter explores one of the most violent, and it expands further the scope of virtual environments presented by exploring* Defiance, *which depicts spontaneously triggered battles with extraterrestrial invaders in the San Francisco area, after the fall of civilization. It also illustrates a very different way in which a gameworld can connect to the wider culture, because it is the twin to a TV series of the same name produced by the SyFy cable channel, interweaving with some of its episodes as they are broadcast. The avatar is based on an exceedingly aggressive corporate executive, one of the founders of a pioneering information technology company, and who served as its CEO for many years. He also was an adventurer in the midst of the First World War, who had a distinctive ethical code somewhat divorced from religion, although he respected Christianity. The avatar sets a goal suitable for the particular sattva, and then discovers that he cannot achieve it by ordinary means. He then turns to serious gaming: tactical choice of actions within a virtual environment, intended to achieve the user's goals but potentially violating the game's design principles.*

Bainbridge, William Sims. *An Information Technology Surrogate for Religion: The Veneration of Deceased Family in Online Games.* New York: Palgrave MacMillan, 2014.
DOI: 10.1057/9781137490599.0005.

DOI: 10.1057/9781137490599.0005

> Gaming: Tactical choice of actions within a virtual environment, intended to achieve the user's goals but potentially violating its design principles.

Defiance is far more emotionally intense than the previous examples, both exceedingly violent and often unpredictable. It also illustrates a very different way in which a gameworld can connect to the wider culture, because it is the twin to a TV series of the same name produced by the SyFy cable channel, interweaving with some of its episodes as they are broadcast. The avatar is based on an exceedingly aggressive corporate executive, Walter Heber Wheeler, Jr. (1897–1974), the nephew of Ernest and June, one of the founders of the Pitney Bowes information technology company in 1920 and who served as its CEO for many years. He also was an adventurer in the midst of the First World War, who had a distinctive ethical code somewhat divorced from religion, although he respected Christianity. A central feature of *Defiance* is sudden alien attacks at unpredictable locations, which require players to combine quickly to counterattack, and which mitigate against thoughtful consideration of alternatives and against development of enduring social relationships or cultural subtleties like religious ritual.

A man with guts and brains

It is said that the Pitney Bowes Corporation, a pioneer in the information technology industry when it was founded in 1920 and with $3.87 billion of revenue in 2013, was created by a trinity.[1] Arthur Pitney was the *inventor*, Walter Bowes was the *entrepreneur*, and Walter Wheeler was the *organizer*. While an oversimplification, this is a nice analysis because it identifies three roles that leaders may play in real life. But Wheeler's role may also be conceptualized in terms of athletic games, because he was a master of strategy and endurance, keeping his eye on the ball and his mind on the goal. Thus, this chapter really concerns two innovative computer games, not merely the early weeks of *Defiance* but also the early years of Pitney Bowes.

On July 30, 2007, Pitney Bowes had a local advertising company upload to YouTube a brief memorial to this hero of high-tech capitalism, in which his own voice can be heard expressing his fundamental philosophy: "Life is essentially a struggle, in one way or another, but without struggle and

DOI: 10.1057/9781137490599.0005

sense of accomplishment, life would be meaningless."[2] I recognized that long-gone voice, because I met him about annually during the 1950s, at family gatherings, either at his home in Stamford, Connecticut, or on his yacht in Long Island Sound.

We called him *Cousin Junior*, and his eldest son, Walter Heber Wheeler III, was called *Tertius*, even by his father, in the tradition of ancient Roman aristocrats. In 1960, he wrote June's son William, who was indeed his cousin: "I think it's high time we dropped the 'cousin.' Plain Junior or Walter will do nicely."[3] Both names, Junior and Walter, connect him to his father, the original Walter Heber Wheeler, the brother of Ernest and June. But, as we shall see, connections to his father became ambiguous, and his mother's intimate choices influenced his public career in an unusual way. I shall continue to call the man Walter, and call his avatar simply Junior, his informatic offspring.

Defiance provided a metaphor for exploring the personal chaos of Walter's early adulthood. Its setting is the San Francisco area in the near future after a catastrophic invasion by extraterrestrials. A goal for Junior is to reach the city itself, where Walter's mother lived in real life, despite the fact that he is unable to defeat the monster that prevents entry by ordinary means. Huge in both body and personality, Walter dominated any group, and he clearly was both aggressive and intelligent. So when aggression could not achieve his goal, he used his intelligence to shape relationships with other people.

Defiance was the first major MMO created in conjunction with a television series, thus bridging between two previously separate electronic media. Of course, *Star Trek Online* was based on a television series, but one that had concluded years earlier. The game version of *Defiance* launched two weeks before the television series in April 2013. The game was produced by Trion Worlds, the same company that produced a very high-quality game named *Rift*, that I had earlier explored, and the television program was produced by SyFy, the science fiction cable network. Frankly, the MMO was a risky endeavor in many ways, and may not have been quite ready when it launched on a schedule determined by the television program. Designed as a "first-person shooter," it emphasized quick reactions in violent environments, a style I am not good at. Logically the sattva should have been someone who had acted forcefully during episodes of grave danger in real life, while being technically sophisticated enough to serve as a vantage point for analyzing the technological innovation of a TV-MMO.

DOI: 10.1057/9781137490599.0005

Walter was the right man for the job. People often distinguish a self-made man from a scion of wealth who inherits his status, but traditionally the dominant males in society tended to be both. Perhaps the clearest description of his nature was one of the first, an article published on December 10, 1916, in the *New York Times*, reporting that he had been unanimously elected captain of the Harvard football team:

> The present season was Wheeler's first of the varsity football squad. He prepared at Wooster Academy, where he played football for two years. An injury in his freshman year kept him out of play until this Fall, when he presented himself to Coach Haughton, and after a hard uphill fight finally clinched the position of left tackle. Wheeler was not rated a regular when the practice started, but in the final six weeks of play advanced with mighty strides. He is tall and rangy, an ideal tackle and weighs 185 pounds. Captain Black after the Yale game, speaking of the new Harvard captain, said: "We found out very early that it was useless to try Wheeler's side of the line for a gain. After that we left him almost entirely alone."
>
> Wheeler's best points are that he is aggressive and can diagnose plays very quickly. It was said that he was the choice of the coaching staff for the position. He is practically without fraternity affiliations and is working his way through college.
>
> The first half of the present year Wheeler spent at Verdun and Alsace driving an ambulance in the American ambulance service. While at the former place he received the Croix de Guerre for carrying the wounded safely to the hospital under a heavy shell fire.

The United States did not enter the First World War until the following year, and the American Volunteer Motor-Ambulance Corps was an organization of Harvard men who believed that America could not remain aloof from the great struggle taking place in Europe. A 1916 book, *The Harvard Volunteers in Europe*, published by Harvard University Press, begins with a poem, the first stanza of which compares war with games:

> From fields of toil and fields of play,
> Wherever surged the game of life,
> All eager for the mightier fray,
> They sped them to the clashing strife.[4]

Letters Cousin Junior wrote to his uncle Ernest, frantically describing the extreme dangers he had experienced in earning the Croix de Guerre, were published anonymous by The American Red Cross Magazine in

DOI: 10.1057/9781137490599.0005

October 1916.[5] In an unpublished memoir of his early life, he described furiously driving an ambulance full of wounded, despite the fact that both rear tires had been blown off by German fire, and commented, "courage is not the absence of fear, but the ability to carry on in spite of it."[6] No wonder he was elected captain of the Harvard football team, yet he did not serve in this responsibility, enlisting in the Navy as soon as the United States entered the war. He earned the Navy Cross as the daring but technically adept captain of a subchaser, which in the First World War required brains as well as guts. I could see what kind of resolute captain he must have been, when I observed him control the three-man paid crew of his 72-foot sailing yacht, Cotton Blossom IV.

However, the story of his involvement in Pitney Bowes had some of the quality of a soap opera, rather than a science fiction adventure story. Cousin Junior's parents became friends with Walter H. Bowes, and over the years his mother Charlotte developed an affair with Bowes, who was much younger than she, and before revealing it prevailed upon her husband to cash in an insurance policy and lend the money to Bowes for his business. A divorce followed, when Junior was in boarding school, and Charlotte married Bowes. His innovative business was providing stamp-cancelling machines for the US Post Office, and in 1920 he teamed up with Arthur Pitney who had patented his first machine of this kind back in 1902. As Wikipedia reports, their goal was "producing a machine that would combine Pitney's 'double-locking' counter with Bowes's system for wrapping postage payment, postmarking and cancellation. The United States Post Office approved their postage meter on August 25, 1920."[7]

Family legend says more, and the official history of the corporation agrees.[8] A crucial meeting was scheduled with officials of the US Post Office, at which Pitney and Bowes would show how their combined system would work, because they needed official approval to have their "mechanical stamps" considered legitimate postage. On the train down to Washington from their headquarters in Stamford, Connecticut, Pitney and Bowes got into a heated argument, and at Union station they separated, each angrily going in a different direction and checking into a different hotel. Junior shuttled back and forth between them, coaxing them to cooperate for the crucial meeting. Pitney died in 1933, and although Bowes survived until 1957, Junior took over the company in 1938. The online Harvard database, "American Business Leaders of the Twentieth Century" says this about him:

DOI: 10.1057/9781137490599.0005

Wheeler served as CEO or Chairman of Pitney-Bowes for over three decades. Under his leadership, Pitney-Bowes grew from a regional postage meter manufacturer generating $3 million in revenues to a $300 million diversified direct mail machinery operation. He presided over a massive investment and diversification program that produced the first mass-market postage meter and a complete line of integrated mail processing equipment. Many of Pitney-Bowes' machines set the standard for the United States Postal Service.[9]

Today, the company calls itself "a leading provider of customer communication technologies." It boasts, "Our software, equipment and services help businesses communicate more effectively in today's multi-channel environment, so they can build long-term customer relationships and drive profitable growth."[10] Throughout its early years, Pitney Bowes had only one line of products, postage meters. This meant that its business plan was to be a monopoly, which had the effect of forcing Walter to find the one exact path through years of litigation and engineering challenges, using brains rather than violence, but very much engaged in a player-versus-player game in which a loss would be equivalent to the death of a business.

In 2007, as if to emphasize the connections between information technology and ethics, a blogger on the Christian Messageboard reported correctly, "Many historians find Walter Wheeler to be a study in contrasts. He admittedly was a hard-nosed executive who was determined to promote his company, yet he instituted some of the most farsighted programs to benefit employees and the public of any company during his era."[11] Many of the anecdotes about his idealism concern fairness for members of minority groups, as he resigned from a prominent social club when he saw it practicing anti-Semitism, took a company meeting out of a hotel that refused to serve a minority employee, and worked on many social-justice causes in Connecticut.

My mother detested him, however. She once explained to me that early in his career with the Equitable Life Assurance Society my father had invested great effort developing a group life insurance plan for Pitney Bowes, but Walter then showed it to other companies and took their lowest bid, in violation of the ethical principle that competing proposals deserve confidentiality. Perhaps he was simply seeking the best deal, or wanted to avoid charges of nepotism, but the episode aggravated already sour family relations, dating back to the affair Charlotte had with Bowes that gave Walter his chance to play the real monopoly game.

DOI: 10.1057/9781137490599.0005

A key role played by religion in traditional societies was arbiter of morals. But it is difficult to find mention of intellectual property rights in the bible. Romans 13:7 is sometimes quoted in support of copyright: "Render therefore to all their dues: tribute to whom tribute is due; custom to whom custom; fear to whom fear; honour to whom honour." But it does not explain how we determine ownership—by whom or for how long.

The final pages of Walter's unpublished memoir is a meditation on religion, in which he honors Christianity as the faith of his fathers, but respects all faiths: "How did man evolve from a primitive beast grabbing, pillaging, taking everything he could by whatever means, into his state today where such things as honesty, courage, fairness, charity, nobility, self-sacrifice, tolerance and love are at least universally recognized in all major religions, however imperfectly practiced? Our very failure to live up to these standards, even our hypocrisy, only proves their existence as a meaningful aspiration of man." This was the man I sent into *Defiance*.

A new Earth

The backstory on which the game and TV show are based is very complex, setting the stage for many game missions and video episodes. In simple terms, an astronomical catastrophe in another solar system sent a fleet of Votan refugees belonging to several alien intelligent species to Earth, bringing with them technologies to transform our planet to their liking, on the assumption that Earth was uninhabited. When they arrived and discovered the truth, a series of attempts to find a peaceful solution failed, and much of Earth was devastated, causing the collapse of civilization. The television program takes place in the town of Defiance, a rag-tag settlement on the ruins of St. Louis, over which the famous arch still rises. The game takes place in the San Francisco area, initially just north of the city. The landscape is ruined, even to the point that the coastline has shifted, and many dangers abound.

Defiance begins with a bang! Junior awakened in the midst of rubble from the crash of a huge 600-passenger stratocarrier, called the New Freedom, into "Mount Tam," the Mount Tamalpais that dominates Marin County. A friendly alien woman named Cass Ducar of the Irathient species helps him get oriented and then asks him to help her with several missions. Junior discovers that he has been implanted with an EGO artificial intelligence guide that sometimes appears as a ghostly, transparent woman, and it takes him a while to realize that both Cass and EGO can be both beneficial and demanding. For a while they look for survivors and try to restore communications systems, battling enemies who belong to gangs. They enter an outpost of the military, with which Junior is remotely affiliated, and the commander decides to interrogate Cass to learn what she knows about the territory, so Junior undertakes a number of minor missions on his own.

The chief avatar statistic in *Defiance* that measures progress is EGO points, which had a cap of 5000, but this number is far above what players could reach without repeating many battles many times. At only level 30, Junior undertook a mission called "A Little Competition," his first experience with an *arkfall*. A *Defiance* Wiki explains what one is: "Wreckage from the Votan ships that exploded in space periodically falls to Earth. These meteor-like fragments usually contain rare and valuable alien technology."[12] Since he was destined to be an *ark hunter*, this was a crucial training experience, and he would face many more much larger arkfalls later. The competition in the mission's title is a pair of fellow ark hunters, a Human man and an Irathient woman, not to mention some small monsters swarming around the meteor that the three of them battle, side by side.

At the end, the man introduces himself, as the woman silently hunts through the wreckage: "Come on. Let's loot this thing before the vultures swoop in. This is fun, right? I'm sure glad you made it off that stratocarrier. Name's Nolan. This little ray of sunshine is Irisa. We got a little job coming up. Maybe we'll be in touch. ... We could use an extra pair of hands. If you're a fan of scrip [money] then meet Irisa and me at the Crater Bar." Nolan and Irisa are the central characters of the television program, the avatars look just like them, and the actors provided the voices for the cutscene quoted above. Presumably, this scene happened some time before the first episode of the show, when Nolan and Irisa arrived at St. Louis, and is one of the most obvious connections. There is something remarkably impressive about collaborating on a mission with realistic artificial intelligence characters whose appearance and even voices make them seem very much like real people.

Junior did meet the pair later, and shared a mission with them called "The Heist," in which they attempted to steal the Libera Nova gem back from the Raiders, which an alien capitalist named Varus Soleptor claimed really belonged to him. Since I watched every episode of the program,

DOI: 10.1057/9781137490599.0005

by that point it was really impressive to be battling enemies in a virtual environment with the two main characters at my side, looking for all the world as if they were alive. But were they Junior's friends? Nolan grabbed the gem, but in the battle Junior was separated from him, and the couple vanished.

In the mission called "The Departed," Varus sent Junior to confront them. Unexpectedly, Irisa jumped Junior, held a knife to his throat, and said, "You're too late. The gem's not here. Neither is Nolan. So go and tell that shtako Varus that he lost." Just then, Nolan called for help, and Junior decided that he would assist the independent couple before blaming them. After a difficult fight, in which Junior had to heal wounds both Nolan and Irisa had suffered, Nolan offered to give the gem to Junior, in addition to a nice rifle, as payment for saving his life. But by sleight of hand, Nolan stole the gem back, and Junior did not realize what had happened until after the couple departed, vaguely saying that they were headed to Antarctica.

Junior's first major arkfall happened when he had reached EGO level 64, perhaps five miles down the highway from his starting point. On the game's map, he could see five red icons representing arkfalls, within a larger red circle maybe a mile across. This was a cluster of falls, of a sort he would see many times in his future. He rode his off-trail vehicle to one of the five arkfalls, where he and a score of other players destroyed one meteor while battling alien hellbugs of various kinds. Once all five minor falls had been eliminated, a huge one appeared to which all the players rushed, where they battled bugs of many kinds, primarily a gigantic Mature Hellbug Hellion whose death ended the mission. The combat seemed to last forever, but checking the time stamps on the screenshots I took, Junior's entire involvement took 16 minutes.

Junior helped Cass fix a damaged radio station, and after some more solo missions, their main goal became Karl von Bach, a passenger on the New Freedom whose company created many of the most powerful weapons used in the war between humans and aliens that led to the fall of both civilizations, and whom she describes as "your boss." They find the escape pod in which he ejected from the New Freedom, with a recorded message saying which direction he was headed and mentioning he possessed an ark-core, the most valuable alien relic. She exclaimed: "Did he just say ark-core? Your boss has an ark-core? Usually I would say let's get it for ourselves and sell it for crazy piles of jaja, but arktech jacked up this planet in the first place. What kind of shtako is he trying to do? We

DOI: 10.1057/9781137490599.0005

better find him before someone kills him. And way more importantly, we need to make sure no one takes that core."

Junior had reached EGO level 119 when they rescued von Bach, and Cass demanded to know his intentions. He explained, "I have no intentions. My promise is to find the ark-matrix and cell needed to get this core working, use it to start up a terra-spire, and then use what I learn to fix this whole damn planet." This consolidates the main mission arc Junior, and every other player, was expected to complete: assemble all three parts of the ark-spire so von Bach could discover a technological solution to the world's problems. Yet this solution sounded rather like a super-weapon that could destroy all enemies or force them into submission to von Bach's personal power. Immediately, Junior faced a dilemma that would weigh on his spirit for the rest of his time in *Defiance*.

Going to San Francisco

Junior's early missions with Cass, saving survivors of the crash of the New Freedom, was a replay of Cousin Junior's service as a volunteer ambulance driver in the First World War. Yet that real-world adventure had its own surreal and amoral aspects. Walter's private memoire revealed he had contracted gonorrhea at the Folies Bergère in Paris, and at one particularly dangerous moment buried his medicine in a field, not wanting it to be sent back with his dead body to his parents, to his posthumous shame. Junior may have flirted with Cass, as Walter did with the Folies dancers, but his main activity was heroic and admirable.

The new mission, to assemble the separated parts of the ark-spire was a replay of the real-life episode in which he mediated between Pitney and Bowes, to reassemble the postage meter for the crucial government demonstration. While not as influential as IBM, Pitney-Bowes was prominent among the companies that developed information technology and gave us the communications systems that today serve our needs, while raising ethical issues around privacy and power. Junior decided to follow the orders given by von Bach, but not because the mission arc was like the one he had dedicated his working life to, but because it could connect him to his wayward but beloved mother. She had been a native of San Francisco, and the only way he could reach her home, passing the monster that blocked the only route, was to complete the main mission arc.

DOI: 10.1057/9781137490599.0005

April 20, 2013, brought a revealing disaster to Junior, when he was at EGO level 325. The first involved the 23rd mission in the main story arc, "A Bullet for a Badman." The description inside the game said: "Enter Dogtown Mine alongside Rosa. Joe Teach has the ark-cell and Rosa wants vengeance for her father's murder." Rosa was a friendly nonplayer character, and without much difficulty she and Junior were able to shoot their way into a chamber where Joe stood high on a platform protected by a high-tech energy shield, as he sent minions to defend his position. Junior was able to kill a few, then was killed himself, rezzing outside the chamber and losing his progress in killing the bad guys. After a couple more deaths, I checked the online forums and learned I should position Junior behind a particular protective barrier, facing enemies only one or two at a time, and following a complex tactic to erode Joe's shield. Junior got further, but still died, each time losing any progress he had achieved. I checked the forums again and found that other people were having this problem, and apparently the battle was simply too difficult for a significant fraction of the players.

I began posting my own view on the forums, including in the bugs section hoping the game programmers would see it: "Several people on the forums have complained they cannot defeat the bosses in A Bullet for a Badman and the final Defiance mission in the first arc. To be sure, you don't want to nerf the game, but given the tie-in to the SyFy series, this game attracts a range of players, including many veteran MMO players like myself who are not able to handle twitch games and may be more oriented to story and exploration—the main features of science fiction—than to competition against other players."

Nerf means excessively reducing the difficulty of something in a game, *twitch* refers to games in which fast reaction times are crucial, and *mobs* are mobile nonplayer characters, in gamer lingo. Having Joe being a difficult boss was consistent with the story, because this was when one of the missing ark pieces could be retrieved, but difficulty can be defined in several ways. One solution would have been to provide a second path forward, more arduous to make it fair, and another was to let a character return to it at an EGO level far above that of the NPC enemies. *Defiance* adjusts the difficulty of mob enemies to match the level of the player, so it is often impossible to complete a mission by returning to it after defeat, much later after gaining more powers. Regretfully, I abandoned "A Bullet for a Badman," losing the progress Rosa and Junior had achieved in getting to the final chamber.

DOI: 10.1057/9781137490599.0005

The real Walter was not a quitter, and would not have been happy to see me quit a crucial mission. Periodically, I retried the mission, always failing, the last time at EGO level 625. In my mind I debated with Junior, telling him von Bach would only use the ark-spire to become dictator of the world, causing even more casualties rather than peace. This argument had some logic, but how could Junior reach his mother's home in San Francisco, if he did not complete the main mission arc?

I discovered a simple hack that turned the trick. One player may invite another to be a friend. Players could teleport to the location of a friend. Unlike the system in many virtual worlds, that requires both parties to agree to the teleport, in *Defiance* friend A could teleport to the location of friend B, without the help of friend B. Then I found that asking someone to become a friend had the effect of establishing a temporary friend link that lasted until the other person rejected it. So I simply used the in-game system for finding potential quest partners, entering common names, until I found a player who was currently in San Francisco. I offered him a friendship, then immediately teleported to his location before he could react. The ultimate result was confirmation that the home of Junior's mother in San Francisco was a wasteland of ashes.

Conclusion

Defiance is extremely interesting, although it fits Junior's skills far better than it did mine, and I was happy to end my exploration two months after it began. Many players raised criticisms in the forums, and it was hard to tell whether they were all justified, or merely expressed the rather hostile temperament of some people who like extremely violent action shooter games. Trion, the company that created *Defiance*, ran into serious financial problems rather immediately, and *Defiance* did not become popular among the wider MMO community. This led the company to close the San Diego office that had created it, moving the game's operations to its headquarters fittingly enough near San Francisco.[13] Pitney-Bowes continues to be a successful information technology corporation, but overshadowed by Google and dozens of other more recent start-ups. Perhaps industrial entrepreneurship is indeed the equivalent of playing a computer game. However well one does, someone else, perhaps playing a new game, will surpass one's accomplishments.

DOI: 10.1057/9781137490599.0005

Notes

1   en.wikipedia.org/wiki/Pitney_Bowes.
2   www.youtube.com/watch?v=PcnQ1v3IhII.
3   Personal letter from Walter H. Wheeler, Jr., to William Wheeler Bainbridge, February 19, 1960.
4   M. A. DeWolfe (ed.), *The Harvard Volunteers in Europe* (Cambridge, MA: Harvard University Press, 1916), Wheeler is mentioned on pp. 205 and 261.
5   Walter Heber Wheeler, Jr. (published anonymously), "Ten Days at Verdun: The Story of an American Ambulance Driver." *The American Red Cross Magazine*, October 1916, 11(10): 335–338.
6   Walter Heber Wheeler, Jr., "Memoirs," edited posthumously by Thomas C. Wheeler, typescript, 1975.
7   en.wikipedia.org/wiki/Pitney_Bowes
8   William Cahn, *The Story of Pitney-Bowes* (New York: Harper, 1961), p. 52.
9   www.hbs.edu/leadership/database/leaders/walter_h_wheeler_jr.html.
10   www.pb.com/our-company/.
11   The Story Teller, Christian Messageboard, May 7, 2007; http://www.christian-messageboard.com/forums/index.php?showtopic=18062.
12   en.defiance-wiki.com/wiki/Arkfall.
13   Tyler Wilde, "Trion Shuts Down Its San Diego Studio," *PCGamer*, August 8, 2013; www.pcgamer.com/2013/08/08/trion-shuts-down-san-diego-studio/.

DOI: 10.1057/9781137490599.0005

4
Seeking Truth (*Tabula Rasa*)

Abstract: *Among the very most intellectually sophisticated gameworlds, one sadly terminated by the profit-hungry company that published it, was* Tabula Rasa. *Set in the near future, it assumed the Earth had been invaded by evil extraterrestrials, and the few human survivors were forced to flee to two distant planets, where they cooperated with friendly natives and began to fight their way back home to Earth. However, the fundamental concept of* Tabula Rasa *was deeply intellectual, rather than crudely violent, based on the philosophy that the human mind is a blank slate* (tabula rasa) *that could gather pieces of knowledge from the environment and assemble them into wisdom. In ancient days, the benevolent Eloh alien species—inspired by the Hebrew Elohim concept—had hidden Logos hieroglyphics, one each in a widely distributed set of shrines, which the avatar should seek. Thus, the fundamental principle of the game was* ontology, *the search for a system of fundamental concepts with which to understand and manipulate reality. The avatar was based on a man who considered himself to be a medical scientist, whose entire life and thoughts are exceedingly well documented, emphasizing lectures he gave at the religious and intellectual resort, Chautauqua, just over a century ago.*

Bainbridge, William Sims. *An Information Technology Surrogate for Religion: The Veneration of Deceased Family in Online Games*. New York: Palgrave MacMillan, 2014. DOI: 10.1057/9781137490599.0006.

> Ontology: The search for fundamental concepts with which to understand and manipulate reality.

Among the very most intellectually sophisticated gameworlds, one sadly terminated by the profit-hungry company that published it, was *Tabula Rasa*. The avatar that explored it was based on William Seaman Bainbridge (1870–1947), a prominent New York surgeon and June's son. He developed all the simulated biological skills offered in the game, while seeking wisdom across the vast territories of two planets. *Tabula Rasa* actually ended with a return not merely to Earth, but to a point in New York City within easy walking distance of the doctor's home and office on Gramercy Park. The fundamental metaphor concerns how science might substitute for religion in discovering the meaning of existence, and how medicine may supplant faith in curing disorders.

Life's Day

Will—as his friends called him in tribute to his willpower during adulthood—was born on February 17, 1870, and his earliest weeks were clouded by the death of his sister Cleora on April 14. He would not have remembered that traumatic event, but his mother Lucy brooded intensely about it, eventually adopting a girl named Helen as a living avatar for Cleora. He accompanied his parents on their 1879–1880 tour of American Protestant missions in Asia, embarking from San Francisco the day after his ninth birthday, and he repeatedly experienced his mother's obsession with death as she explored the tombs and observed the funeral practices of many exotic peoples. Even before reaching their first destination in Japan, he watched his clergyman father practice missionary proselytization on 600 Chinese laborers traveling in steerage. Half a dozen of them died during the weeks the ship ploughed westward, but even in death, they longed to return home. By paying the ship's doctor 40 dollars for his work and a bottle of carbolic acid, each arranged to be pickled so his body could be buried in China.

Will's own closest brush with premature death came when he was already a medical student at Columbia University and contracted typhoid fever. This bacterial infection is a form of corrupt contamination, typically caused by drinking water that contains feces from an infected person, and it has largely vanished from civilized nations today because

DOI: 10.1057/9781137490599.0006

of improvements in the water supply. In typhoid, the victim's tempera-
ture slowly rises over a period of weeks until it reaches 104° Fahrenheit
or higher. Other symptoms are headache, abdominal pain, weakness,
diarrhea, rose-colored spots on the chest, nosebleeds, and even intestinal
bleeding. The progress of typhoid can be very slow, and a victim who
recovers may be a carrier of the disease for months. A generation before
Will contracted it, Lucy's dear brother George did, and that episode
intensified the emotions around Will's case. George and Lucy were very
close, and he begged his sister "Lutey," as he had called her in childhood,
to stay with him and tend him in his illness. This she did, caring for him,
praying with him, and singing to him every day until his death.

Lucy tended Will with great devotion a generation later, remembering the horrible days she tended her brother George as the same disease
gradually killed him. Doctors had learned that microorganisms in
contaminated water were the cause of typhoid, but as yet they had no
cure. For weeks, Will lay in delirium, aware he might soon die. Recovery
was terribly slow, and he fell far behind his Columbia University class-
mates. At the same time, Lucy and her clergyman husband were going
through the worst stage of marital estrangement, as he was failing to
fulfill his pastoral duties and spiraling downward into esoteric scholarly
obsessions. Will was so ashamed of his father's apparently willful failure
that he considered renouncing the name Bainbridge, but did not follow
through on this dire idea. Thus, Will was struggling against both death
and dishonor simultaneously, in an episode that powerfully shaped his
character. One superficial result was that he became a leader in efforts
to clean up water supplies, but the more profound results can only be
imagined.

Despite the fact that he died on September 22, 1947, three weeks before
my seventh birthday, I remember him well. My last memory of him was
visiting him on his deathbed to say goodbye. He knew very well he was
dying, and understood the significance of every one of his symptoms.
His spiritual guide was Norman Vincent Peale, advocate of the power of
positive thinking.[1] Peale believed that the philosophy he shared with his
medical friend "enables people to gain great victories over that harshest
of all realities." He wrote that Dr. Bainbridge was "a big, aggressive man,
strong and with boundless energy." But age and infirmity had brought
him near to death, and none of his skill or science could save him. His
son, William, in perhaps the most agonizing duty of his life, carried
heavy tanks of oxygen out to Connecticut on the train from New York,

DOI: 10.1057/9781137490599.0006

to prolong his father's life. But the end neared. According to Peale, the faith of this "great scientist and great physician" remained firm until the last, as did that of his wife. They did not discuss the approach of death until the very day he died. Expressing his last professional judgment, he said, "I might not get well."

June replied, "O that I might go with you on this last journey as I have on so many of the others! If you now get over to the other country ahead of me, wait around for me, will you?"

His voice had been weak, and consciousness was fading from him, but in a suddenly strong voice he spoke his last words, "I'll be waiting for you. I'll be there."[2]

Yet Peale's book is not the right document to glean Will's conception of his own, personal death. Better is Will's own early book, *Life's Day*, published in 1909, especially the concluding chapter, titled "Night," which concerns death. The very last sentence of the book quotes poetess Anna Laetitia Barbauld: "Say not 'Good-night,' but in some brighter clime Bid me 'Good-morning.'" *Life's Day* was written for a popular audience, and lacks footnotes and bibliography, yet googling these words allowed identification of the author.[3] Will gave an author's name, Dr. W. W. Keen, when quoting his view that death should be "not the last enemy, but our best friend." But unless we search Internet for the original, we will not know that Keen was writing from a devout Christian perspective, seeing death as the doorway to a glorious afterlife.[4] Will refrained from proclaiming his own Christian faith, allowing his readers to infer it, but aware that their own beliefs might be somewhat different from his own.

The "Night" chapter of *Life's Day* contains another definition: *death is the price human beings must pay for their complexity.* It is difficult to think of a more profound idea than this, and it comes not from Christianity but from the scientific revolution that was already some decades advanced a century ago. Will quotes Charles Minot, but without a footnote to guide us. Searching online locates a remarkable series of essays about aging in the context of biological evolution, that observes that each single-celled organism is in a sense thousands of years old, if not millions, given that they do not have offspring but divide such that each "child" is also the "parent." Biological evolution has rendered complexity possible, including that ultimate complication, intelligence, but with this price:

> Differentiation leads up, as its inevitable conclusion, to death. Death is the price we are obliged to pay for our organization, for the differentiation which exists in us. Is it too high a price? To that organization we are indebted for the

DOI: 10.1057/9781137490599.0006

great array of faculties with which we are endowed. To it we are indebted for the means of appreciating the sort of world, the kind of universe, in which we are placed. To it we are indebted for all the conveniences of existence, by which we are able to carry on our physiological processes in a far better and more comfortable manner than can the lower forms of life. To it we are indebted for the possibility of those human relations which are among the most precious parts of our experience. And we are indebted to it also for the possibility of the higher spiritual emotions.[5]

The wider context in which *Life's Day* was written also juxtaposes religion with science. The book is a compilation of lectures that Will gave at The Chautauqua Institution. Chautauqua was founded in 1874 by two Methodists, clergyman John Heyl Vincent and businessman-inventor Lewis Miller. Initially they intended only to create a summer training institute for Sunday School teachers, but soon it was a complex mix of correspondence courses, branch Chautauquas, and a summer center that presented every manner of cultural uplift. The Chautauqua movement asserted that the whole of life should be a school and that the true basis of education was religion. Miller wrote, "Chautauqua was founded for an enlarged recognition of the Word." There, inquiring people of every denomination could "with square and plumb, with compass and sundial, with telescope and microscope, with steam-engine and telegraph, with laboratory and blackboard, with hammer and spade, search out the deep and hidden mysteries of the Book."[6]

For Vincent, "All knowledge becomes glorified in the man whose heart is consecrated to God."[7] "Away with this dividing up of things! All things that are legitimate are of God. The human intellect belongs to God, and it is to be cultivated for him."[8] "Look through microscopes, but find God. Look through telescopes, but find God. Look for him revealed in the throbbing life about you, in the palpitating stars above, in the marvelous records of the earth beneath you, and in your own souls."[9] When Will was still a teenager, his family began summering at Chautauqua, where he became inspired by Dr. Jay W. Seaver, a pioneer of anthropometry, the science of measuring the human body. As a systematic form of examination, coupled with scientific gymnastics, anthropometry promised physical excellence.[10]

The 1892 session centered on a great National Pageant to mark the four hundredth anniversary of the Voyage of Columbus. Six thousand people crowded the amphitheater to hear chorus and orchestra perform national airs and to see ten historical tableaus. As if to express his vast

DOI: 10.1057/9781137490599.0006

ambitions, Will took the role of Columbus. As documented by photographs in the family's collection, his costume was a mass of robes, an irregular ruffled collar that flowed down the front of his herringbone vest, and a huge wig. Underneath he wore his Pilgrim costume for a later tableau, consisting of a black coat with a more regular white collar and a vast square belt buckle with matching buckled shoes. The following year he completed his medical training at Columbia, many rich New Yorkers who visited Chautauqua became his year-round patients, and he began giving lectures that evolved into _Life's Day_.[11]

On Independence Day, July 4, 2008, Will began a new role, a doctor who was both a Columbus and a Pilgrim, named Bridgebain in _Tabula Rasa_ (TR). _Bridgebain_ was his real-world "email" (telegraph) address in 1923 when he undertook a self-assigned mission against the Germans, inspecting the conditions in the Ruhr and Rhineland territories that his friends the French and Belgians had occupied in response to German failure to pay its debts from World War I.[12] _Tabula Rasa_ was a philosophically complex virtual world, killed off in 2009 because it had not proved profitable, ideal for revival of Will because it believed as he did that simple truths were hidden across the universe, simultaneously scientific and spiritual, awaiting discovery.

A blank slate

Like _Defiance_, _Tabula Rasa_ depicts defensive human military action in the face of an alien invasion, but it has an utterly different ethos, offering a plausible techno-religion. In ancient days, an advanced alien species called the _Eloh_ (cf. Hebrew _Elohim_ meaning _gods_) archived all the secrets of the universe, one in each of a myriad of hidden shrines, to be discovered by spiritually sophisticated explorers from less-advanced intelligent species. But an evil offshoot of the Eloh, the _Neph_ (cf. Hebrew _Nephilim_ meaning _demigods_), is using some of that knowledge to conquer the galaxy, and a few thousand humans have escaped a devastated Earth, seeking to regroup and form alliances before retaking their world.

The chief creator of _Tabula Rasa_, Richard Garriott, had played that same role in developing _Ultima Online_, one of the very first MMOs that launched way back in 1997. The son of astronaut Owen Garriott, he infused TR with a pro-spaceflight ideology, and more deeply with a conception that the universe was meaningful but we had not yet discovered many of its most profound secrets. In gameplay and graphics, TR was about equal to the other top-quality MMOs of its period, yet it was never popular and the company that published it shut it down when Garriott was returning to Earth from an actual spaceflight, having paid millions of dollars to visit the International Space Station. Many explanations might be offered for TR's failure. Yet it is hard to avoid the conclusion that most game players are uninterested in philosophical speculations, and failed to appreciate TR's best qualities.

Ten thousand years ago, the Eloh sought to share their wisdom with lesser species, helping some but eventually leading to chaos and the formation of the Neph who built an evil interstellar army called the Bane. Early in the twenty-first century, the Bane invaded Earth, causing a wave of refugees to flee to other planets, carrying Bridgebain to the verdant planet Foreas. He joined a resistance against the Bane, in the form of a Human army assisted by the natives, called the Allied Free Sentients.

The first quest Bridgebain completed at level 1 of experience was a simple demolition mission, opening the way for further progress, and at level 2 he completed one with the Latin title "Carpe Diem"—seize the day. The philosophical meaning was obvious: one must overcome barriers to achieve goals, and the greatest barrier as well as resource is time. At level 3, Brigadier General Beacham of the AFS told Bridgebain that their first grand goal was to liberate Foreas, then the volcanic planet Arieki, then Mycon. Neither of them could know that *Tabula Rasa* itself would be destroyed before anyone even reached Mycon. This difficult lesson would take months to learn, although it is already implied by *carpe diem*. One must seize the day because the days of a human life are numbered, and some deeply desired goals will never be reached.

Bridgebain met the humanoid inhabitants of Foreas, and began to learn about their religion, which intertwined with their factual knowledge about the Eloh. One of the Foreans, Logos Mentor Ensine, told him: "There is much to learn in our universe. To learn the gift of Logos is to learn awareness and, thus, being. I can be your guide in your Logos journey, and together we may open your essence to enlightenment. The Benefactor Shrines teach us more about the power of Logos. Searching for them is both an honor and a privilege. Often the Shrines can be found deep within the earth. I know of two caves in this vicinity, and both can be found near cascading waters." Oddly, most human members of the AFS were uninterested in the Logos wisdom, but Bridgebain was more sensitive, and resolved to expand his knowledge and his consciousness.

DOI: 10.1057/9781137490599.0006

So now, reincarnated as Bridgebain, Will would explore Foreas and Arieki, completing many missions assigned by the AFS, but primarily seeking to learn for himself all he could about Eloh science. In many remote locations on both planets, inspecting an Eloh shrine gave him one of the Logos hieroglyphics, and thus a fragment of their knowledge and their power. The name of the game, *Tabula Rasa*, refers to the blank slate of an inexperienced human mind, but also to the *tabula* into which the hieroglyphics are collected. One of the game's advertising slogans expresses a different shade of meaning: "A New Beginning… A Clean Slate." Departure from Earth transformed humanity, like graduation from primary school, or even a religious conversion.

Assembled into sentences, the Logos hieroglyphs unlocked advanced abilities, depending upon which military specialty the avatar had. Naturally, Bridgebain had selected a path toward ever-increasing medical technology, and eventually became an exobiologist, with the hieroglyphs needed to spell the sentence that would create a temporary clone of himself to fight alongside him. In a few situations, enemies created clones of Will that attacked him. A clone can also be a religious symbol, a blessing or a curse, a transmigration of the soul or split personality, metempsychosis or psychosis.

Every avatar began duty on Foreas in the *recruit* rank, and then at level 5 of the 50 experience levels had a choice of going down one of two paths, *soldier* or *specialist.* At level 15, a soldier could become either a commando or a ranger, and a specialist could become either a sapper or a biotechnician. At level 30, the categories expanded to eight: grenadier, guardian, sniper, spy, demolitionist, engineer, medic, and exobiologist. At each branch point, the player could save a clone of the avatar, making it possible to return later on and use that clone to explore a different range of abilities that would employ the Logos hieroglyphics in different ways. Other MMOs have complex, hierarchical systems of class development, but this one seemed intellectually rather sophisticated, separating action classes from more intellectual classes, and allowing the Bridgebain avatar to find the path most suited for his sattva.

Bridgebain did indeed collect all of the Logos hieroglyphs and reach level 50 of experience, but *Tabula Rasa* was shut down before I could return to explore more of the specialties of the clones I had saved at the branch points. Admirably, as it was shutting down, TR gave the few remaining players the opportunity to return to Earth for a battle against the Bane. The exact location was remarkably meaningful for Bridgebain,

DOI: 10.1057/9781137490599.0006

because it was Madison Square Park in Manhattan, not far from Gramercy Park where Will had his home and office for a half century. However, he arrived on the battlefield alone, never really having joined a group of other players, and unable to join one now in the game's last days, so he could not reach his old home, and Bridgebain was killed by the Bane.

Fragments of wisdom

I have written at length about *Tabula Rasa* in earlier publications, but there is something even deeper about it that deserves consideration.[13] Perhaps its most fanciful assumption, one shared by much science fiction, is that there remain secrets about existence that can be learned by science and applied through technology. This was always the hope of alchemy, to find a way to transform lead into gold, sinners into saints.[14] Perhaps almost all the truths of science have already been discovered, and the utmost care is required to exploit the last few discoveries without causing more harm than good.

Each Logos shrine added a hieroglyph to the avatar's tabula, allowing its use in a sentence that could be compared with a magic spell, but might better be conceptualized as a computer program, in which each hieroglyph represented a procedure or a variable. Each hieroglyph was written in white inside a black square, and many were pictographs that humans could easily interpret. For example, *feeling* was a stylized heart, *is* was an equal sign, and *time* was an hourglass. At the end of his research, Bridgebain possessed a full collection of all the hieroglyphs in the game, and I took screenshots of all these symbols with definitions and of many sentences in the Logos language. Presumably, the planet Mycon would have offered more shrines, and had it been commercially successful TR could have accessed many other worlds. That raises a painful double question: How many truths exist? What faction of those truths can humans ever discover?

All classes of character needed distinctive Logos hieroglyphs to gain class-specific skills, as well as more general ones such as *power* that gave recruits the ability to cast lightning bolts at enemies. This system of artificial abilities can be understood, and insights into humanity's position in the real universe can be suggested, by comparing the five main skill-lines of exobiologists with those of engineers. Although Bridgebain was

DOI: 10.1057/9781137490599.0006

an exobiologist, the interface allowed me to inspect the abilities of other classes, so the following is based on screenshots I took inside the game, as well as on information in the instruction manual that came with TR. Below are descriptions of the five special formulas for exobiologists, plus similar ones employed by engineers, with translations of the individual hieroglyphs in brackets:

EXOBIOLOGIST:

Create Clone (Doppelganger): Creates a battle-capable temporary clone of the exobiologist.
      [I, Me][Friend][Summon][Here]
Reanimation: Turns a corpse into a temporary ally.
      [Summon][Life][Negative, Subtract][Spirit]
Reanimation Wave: Reanimates all enemy corpses within the area.
      [Vortex][Life][Negative, Subtract][Spirit]
Cadaver Immolation: Detonates a fallen enemy inflicting damage to nearby foes.
      [Damage][Area][Around][Death]
Hortimonculus: Creates a stationary healing plant.
      [Summon][Life][Control][Friend]

ENGINEER:

Bot Construction: Assembles robots that have varying functionality on the battlefield.
      [Create][Machine][Life][Here]
Turret: Deploys a turret that fires at any nearby targets.
      [Summon][Machine][Damage][Enemy]
Trap: Similar to a turret, but it explodes if enemies attack it.
      [Trap][Damage][Summon][Machine]
Base Wave: Supports nearby allies by improving their armor and damage resistance.
      [Vortex][Repair][Defend][Friend]
Temporary Wormhole: Creates a temporary waypoint to which allies may travel.
      [Friend][Teleport][Machine][Summon]

Bridgebain often used the Create Clone action, less often Reanimation, but not the others, because these two were both easy to manage and intellectually interesting. As he progressed up the experience learning curve, the clone became more effective in two ways. First, the clone was a copy of himself, but at a lower level of experience. When he could first create one, it was 5 levels lower, but at maximum quality just 1 level lower. Second, the duration of the clone increased, from one minute to three. The clone was a copy not merely of himself, but also of his equipment, including armor and weapons. Thus it was possible for Bridgebain to hold one weapon, create a clone that would also hold that weapon, then switch himself to a different weapon so that he and the clone would have somewhat different abilities.

While each of the five skills of the exobiologist or engineer requires possession of the correct Logos hieroglyphics, that is not sufficient. Depending on the skill, some kind of consumable resource is also necessary, constituting the raw material that the Logos sentence uses. Three resources were fundamental to the character: health, power, and adrenaline. Health and power regenerate naturally over time. Health is drained by being wounded by enemies, and loss of all health results in death, which is temporary but has some costs. Power is used for most skills, including Create Clone for exobiologists, and Bot Construction, which is the comparable skill for engineers. Remarkably, a *Tabula Rasa* Wiki survived years longer than the game itself, and provides a nice explanation of adrenaline:

> Adrenaline is a value like health and power. Like power, it is used to activate certain abilities. Some adrenaline-powered abilities (like sprint) slowly drain adrenaline while they are in use. Others use it in chunks, similar to the way power is used. Each of the tier 4 classes also has one signature ability that requires a full bar of adrenaline to activate. Adrenaline is accumulated as you kill enemies in battle. Loss of adrenaline is one of *Tabula Rasa's* death penalties. Upon resuscitation after death, the entire adrenaline bar is drained.[15]

Of course the skills of exobiologist and engineer really are technological in nature, and objective rather than being fantasies. But the technology is computer science, and the realism is virtual. Bridgebain's ability that consumed his full supply of adrenaline was Reanimation Wave, a powerful action that for sake of the gameplay could be used only rarely, after already killing many enemies. Thus one constraint was the logic of the game, rather than the natural laws of the universe. An engineer used adrenaline for Base Wave, and a guidebook explains how that powerful skill fits into the strategy of combat in which several players combine to form a team:

> Base Wave helps your group tank-up for a major battle. For an entire minute, nearby allies get impressive resistance to all damage types. Armor

DOI: 10.1057/9781137490599.0006

regeneration also improves by a huge factor. Save Base Wave for large fights against either a huge number of foes or a single enemy of immense power. It helps to prevent sudden deaths in the group, and it frees healing classes for more offensive combat.[16]

How does this all relate to real-world technology, specifically to technologies of the future that might produce artificial human beings or deliver natural humans to distant stars? At best, it does so only as hope and metaphor. Yes, if may be possible to clone a human being, but that would require the full two-decade process of gestation and maturation that transforms a single egg cell into an adult person. A realistic biological clone would not automatically possess the same weapons and armor as the original person of which it was a copy. That would require the same tedious manufacturing work as the original equipment.

Spaceflight in the real universe has proven technically very difficult. Chemical rockets can just barely loft satellites into orbit, and even transport human to the Moon, but at vast cost. Nuclear-powered rockets are feasible, but present terrible technical difficulties not to mention pollution risks that will render nuclear launch to orbit politically unacceptable. The artificial wormholes created by engineers in *Tabula Rasa* are a form of the standard means for long-distance travel in MMOs, including many of the science fiction games. Yes, a familiar real-world form of teleportation already exists, and it is the hyperlinks in web pages. One can easily teleport from one part of a computer's memory to another, but not from one physical location to another.

Conclusion

In his medical practice and many scientific publications, William Seaman Bainbridge expressed faith that the fundamental causes of disease were few and simple, thus hopeful that comprehensive cures could be discovered.[17] However, a century has passed since he published his magnum opus, *The Cancer Problem*, and cure has proved more difficult than he had imagined.[18] However, he had held the view that cancer was not one disease but several, and the principle that death was the price we pay for our complexity also testifies to the sophistication of his thought. The fact that *Tabula Rasa* died before his avatar could discover all the secrets of the universe seems fitting, as does the fact that he was devoutly religious. Perhaps science borrowed from religion the notion that the cosmos was

DOI: 10.1057/9781137490599.0006

meaningful, and with God's grace all of that meaning would eventually be revealed to humans. This logic suggests that loss of faith in God could eventually cause loss of faith in science, unless scientific research continued to impress us with meaningful discoveries.

Notes

1   Norman Vincent Peale and Smiley Blanton, *The Art of Real Happiness* (Englewood Cliffs, NJ: Prentice-Hall, 1950), pp. 200–202.
2   "Dr. Wm. Seaman Bainbridge, Surgeon, Humanitarian," typescript obituary press release, September 22, 1947; Dr. William S. Bainbridge Dies; Surgeon and Cancer Authority, *New York Herald Tribune*, September 23, 1947; "William Seaman Bainbridge," *Science*, October 3, 1947, 106(2753): 314.
3   Francis Turner Palgrave (ed.), *The Golden Treasury* (New York: Dutton, 1907), p. 194.
4   William Williams Keen, *Addresses and Other Papers* (Philadelphia: Saunders, 1905), p. 398.
5   Charles Sedgwick Minot, "The Problem of Age, Growth, and Death," *Popular Science Monthly*, November 1907, 71: 472.
6   Lewis Miller, "Introduction," in *The Chautauqua Movement*, edited by John H. Vincent (Freeport, NY: Books for Libraries Press, 1971; first published 1885), p. v; Theodore Morrison, *Chautauqua* (Chicago: University of Chicago Press, 1974).
7   John H. Vincent, *The Chautauqua Movement* (Freeport, NY: Books for Libraries Press, 1971; first published 1885), p. 87.
8   Ibid., p. 89.
9   Ibid., p. 91.
10 Jay W. Seaver, *Anthropometry and Physical Examination* (New Haven, CT: Tuttle, Morehouse and Taylor, 1890).
11 William Seaman Bainbridge, surviving typescripts and transcriptions of Chautauqua lectures: "Our Bodily Mansion," July 16, 1901; "Helps and Hindrances in the Development of the Child," July 22, 1905; "Lecture by Dr. W. S. Bainbridge at the Hall of Philosophy," July 31, 1903; "Address by Dr. W. S. Bainbridge at the Disciples' House," August 8, 1904; "The Common Disease of the Avenue and the Alley," August 12, 1905.
12 William Seaman Bainbridge, *A Report on Present Conditions in the Ruhr and Rhineland* (New York: Commandery, Military Order of Foreign Wars, November 1923).
13 William Sims Bainbridge, "Science, Technology, and Reality in *The Matrix Online* and *Tabula Rasa*," in *Online Worlds: Convergence of the Real and the Virtual* (London: Springer, 2010), pp. 57–70; "Tabula Rasa," in *The Virtual*

DOI: 10.1057/9781137490599.0006

Future (London: Springer, 2011), pp. 35–54; *eGods* (New York: Oxford University Press), see index.

14　Mircea Eliade, *The Forge and the Crucible* (New York: Harper, 1962).

15　tabularasa.wikia.com/wiki/Adrenaline.

16　Michael Lummis, *Richard Garriott's Tabula Rasa* (Indianapolis: DK Publishing, 2007), p. 91.

17　William Sims Bainbridge, *Personality Capture and Emulation* (London: Springer, 2014), pp 118–123.

18　William Seaman Bainbridge, *The Cancer Problem* (New York: Macmillan, 1914).

DOI: 10.1057/9781137490599.0006

5

Combatting Heresy
(*Perfect World*)

▶

Abstract: *Through history, religion has been as much a battleground as a paradise. Therefore, despite the high level of mutual tolerance exhibited by university scholars of religious studies, one chapter of this book needed to explore hostility. It recounts an* invasion, *a strategic attack against a despised alien culture, conducted as a scouting expedition into a virtual world based on it. The sattva for the avatar is an infant girl, who died in 1870 at the age of one, and was the daughter of two aggressive missionaries who wrote extensively about the world tour they took in 1879–1880. Thus, this chapter has two themes: (1) how it is possible to revive symbolically a person who died in early childhood and thus left little information about personal characteristics, and (2) how it may sometimes be necessary to embrace rather than shun religious conflict. The MMO is* Perfect World, *a Chinese fantasy gameworld containing much Taoist culture. The infant girl's Baptist clergyman father despised Taoism, as her mother despised Chinese culture in its treatment of women, both of them publishing books about their experiences that were highly critical of Asian societies. Thus, her avatar is a vehicle for exploration of religious conflict.*

Bainbridge, William Sims. *An Information Technology Surrogate for Religion: The Veneration of Deceased Family in Online Games.* New York: Palgrave MacMillan, 2014.
DOI: 10.1057/9781137490599.0007.

> Invasion: A strategic attack against a despised alien culture, conducted as a scouting expedition into a virtual world based on it.

Perfect World is a Chinese fantasy gameworld, experienced in its westernized form by an avatar based on Cleora Emily Bainbridge (1868–1870), the sister of the doctor described in the previous chapter. She died about when her brother was born. Had she lived, she would have accompanied their parents, as her brother did, on a two-year world tour of American Protestant missions in Asia, spending many months in China in 1879 at the mission of John Nevius. But the extensive religious content of *Perfect World* is Taoist, and their Baptist clergyman father despised Taoism, as their mother despised Chinese culture in its treatment of women, both of them publishing books about their experiences that were highly critical of Asian societies. Thus, this chapter has two themes: (1) how it is possible to revive symbolically a person who died in early childhood and thus left little information about personal characteristics, and (2) how it may sometimes be necessary to embrace rather than shun religious conflict.

An infant angel

Cleora Emily Bainbridge was born on November 8, 1868 to parents who were religious leaders, and she died on April 14, 1870 of water on the brain. From its very origins, the Christianity in which her parents placed their faith had been concerned with the issue of death. Even modern secularists have good reason to believe that a man named Jesus lived two millennia ago, taught valuable lessons, then unjustly died on the cross. We may doubt that he was subsequently resurrected and awaits his faithful followers in Heaven, when their own time comes. We also may doubt that through a self-sacrificial death he paid for our sins, but it is interesting to note that in its poetic sophistication, Christianity both denies death and justifies death.

It was only by consulting the death records of the state of Rhode Island that I learned Cleora had died of water on the brain. Presumably she suffered from some form of hydrocephalus, which most likely could be treated today by surgically inserting a shunt to drain away excess fluid. But back in 1870, the only response for her parents was to pray. One photograph of Cleora still exists, and it shows an apparently normal

DOI: 10.1057/9781137490599.0007

girl aged about one, sitting comfortably with open eyes. The picture is a tintype, and for years the photographic emulsion has been flaking off from the metal backing. Rather than try to repair the tintype, I scanned it in into my computer, and Oxford University Press was kind enough to post it on its blogsite.[1] That is a nice metaphor for the entire project reported in this book, a tiny example of revival via online virtualization.

In *eGods*, the book about the religious implications of computer games that I published with Oxford, Cleora was the sattva for the avatar that explored *EverQuest 2* (EQII), one of the highest-quality MMO role-playing games. Of course, I had no information about what she actually had thought about religion, because she did not live to an age when she could have articulated her beliefs, let alone have a range of life experiences. The virtual environment is a world named Norath, whose gods have abandoned the inhabitants during a catastrophic crisis when divine help would have been most valuable, but now the gods are creeping back, not to help, but to exploit people for their own selfish purposes. Can we accuse the Christian God of similarly having abandoned Cleora to a premature death?

As I wrote in *eGods*, "To study the ambivalent relationship between gods and humans in EQII, I decided to base my avatar on a real person in my own family whose life was closely related to religion, yet who had a legitimate grievance against God."[2] Thus, as she ascended 80 levels of game experience in EQII, Cleora helped me think about the behavior of the gods, but this did not require me to know how the real Cleora really would have judged them. I was using her as a symbol of ambivalence.

Yet Cleora's appearance in *EverQuest II* was far from her first revival, which took place way back in 1883, when her grieving father wrote a novel titled *Self-Giving*, based on the world tour of Asian missions that she would have experienced had she lived. William Folwell Bainbridge and Lucy Seaman Bainbridge, undertook an extensive tour of American Protestant missions in Japan, China, India and other parts of Asia, covering 50,000 miles over the two full years 1879–1880. William was a Baptist minister who published two serious books reporting his observations, both communicated through vivid anecdotes and enlightened by sociological theory, *Around the World Tour of Christian Missions: A Universal Survey* (1882) and *Along the Lines at the Front: A General Survey of Baptist Home and Foreign Missions* (1882). Lucy was a leader of the Temperance Movement who also published two books, with a slightly more personal focus, and also intellectually quite solid, *Round the World Letters* (1882)

DOI: 10.1057/9781137490599.0007

and *Jewels from the Orient* (1920). Today, these books are available online, and they allow us to understand what Cleora would have experienced in fine detail, had she lived to accompany her parents on both of these remarkable voyages.

A novel revival

Self-Giving tells the story of two Cleoras, both of whom die in religious contexts during Protestant missionary work in India. The real world also had two Cleoras, because Lucy had named her daughter after her mother, Cleora Augusta Seaman (1814–1869), a woman doctor whom Lucy memorialized in an article in the *Medical Woman's Journal* and in her own autobiography.[3] The novel begins when the heroine, Cleora Lyddell, is about the age Cleora Bainbridge would have been when the novel was published, and it says: "She was a real mother's child, already showing the same common sense and personal magnetism. Life being spared, she was sure to make her mark with both head-work and heart-work..." The powerful phase "life being spared" suggests that in fact life was not spared, and death prevented fulfillment of such promise.

As the story progresses, Cleora Lyddell marries Llewellyn Litchfield, and the couple goes to Agra in India to set up a Protestant mission. As William Folwell Bainbridge says in his preface, most incidents in the novel are based in facts, and this may have contributed to problems the author faced in his later career, because many of the incidents are about misbehavior by real people involved in the overseas missionary movement. Indeed, the book is rather arrogant in tone, and the protagonists seem to be idealized versions of Lucy and William themselves. Thus, while I prefer to see Cleora Lyddell as a symbolic expression of lost hopes for Cleora Bainbridge, the character also represents the real character of Lucy Bainbridge, including her hatred of Hindu and Moslem religion for their mistreatment of women, and in the case of Hinduism of members of the lower castes.

We could say that the meaning of a literary symbol is never entirely certain, and poetry cannot be translated perfectly into prose. But perhaps more salient here is the insight that no real person is entirely separate from other members of the family or close associates outside it. The real Cleora would have grown up to have a somewhat independent

DOI: 10.1057/9781137490599.0007

personality, yet also to reflect characteristics of her mother. Thus, Cleora Lyddell can be Cleora Bainbridge, at the same time as being Lucy Bainbridge. And I can be either of them, while remaining myself, through avatars representing them. The daughter in the novel, Cleora Litchfield, is more purely a representation of Cleora Bainbridge. We can imagine, but not know for sure, that the following paragraph described the life of the real Cleora:

> It was a very delicate child. The mother had had to work too hard, and of late under too great a burden of disappointment and anxiety. Half of the time, the first year of the little life, the baby was ill, and when she became old enough to notice objects and to show preferences, it was very evident that no one could relieve the mother so much of the infant's care as the father. Then, Cleora had a long run of fever, and many, many times Llewellyn found it necessary to sit up with her all night.[4]

The climax of the story for little fictional Cleora comes when she is a few years older than the real Cleora ever got to be, able to talk and express her own religious beliefs. It takes place inside the Taj Mahal, the famous Islamic mausoleum built to commemorate Mumtaz Mahal, wife of Shah Jahan, who died while giving birth to their fourteenth child. In her 1882 book, *Round the World Letters*, Lucy called it "The most exquisitely beautiful tomb in all the world, and built by the emperor of a people who despise women, and whose holy book does not recognize that they possess souls."[5] Four times Lucy saw the Taj: once at dawn, once at midday, once in the night when blue lights transformed the interior into sapphire, and finally at sunset when it appeared from the distance like pearl.

Standing alone inside that resonant dome, Lucy sang out a defiant hymn: "In the cross of Christ I glory towering o'er the wrecks of time!" Half a world from home, she stood proud in her faith. "It was a simple air, sung by an untrained voice, but as the sounds were caught up, and repeated by the unseen choir, the impurity seemed to be lost, and, from the dim heights of the vast marble space above, it returned in an echo, soft and sweet and clear."[6]

That unseen choir was the famous long-delay echo, described in the current website of the government of India dedicated to the Taj: "Even sound was put to the task of eternity, through one of the longest echoes of any building in the world."[7] In his novel, William extended that echo at length, describing daughter Cleora's death scene for several pages, as

DOI: 10.1057/9781137490599.0007

she sang, "I want to be an angel," and the echo responded, "Be an angel."[8]
Finally, coughing blood but still singing, she uttered her last words:

O, mamma, papa, they be truly angels now!
—truly angels now!
Mamma, they all look beautiful as you,
—beautiful as you.
They'll take me right to Jesus' arms,
—to Jesus's arms.
And you will both come soon,
—both come soon.
Singing!
—Singing!
Angels of Jesus!
—Angels of Jesus![9]

There are many valid ways to analyze the Christian belief that innocent children may become angels in Heaven at death. Whether bereaved parents fully believe this myth or not, public acceptance of the idea reduces their sense of shame for not having prevented the death of their child. In comparison with Ancient Egyptian religion, for example, Christianity is economically efficient, requiring no costly mummification or tomb. In comparison with the religious situation in most parts of Asia, Christianity unifies very diverse human urges, at least superficially, in a way that the division of labor among Confucianism (ethics), Taoism (magic), and Buddhism (philosophy) does not. Specifically, Christianity greatly reduced the role of magic and magicians, and asserted that the universe possessed intelligible meaning, both of which may have encouraged the emergence of science.[10] Many non-Christian cultural traditions, promote the idea that deceased spirits may return to Earth, a notion that is heavily exploited by many MMOs, *Perfect World* among them.[11]

An imperfect world

There was no better way for Cleora's avatar to visit a virtual China than to explore *Perfect World International* (PWI), the English-language version of a high-quality Chinese gameworld that blends traditional culture with fantasy. The goal was not for Cleora to become Chinese, and settle down in this new realm. Nor was it for her to be merely a tourist passing through quickly and gaining only the most superficial impressions, but somewhere between these two extremes. Because she was not an immi-grant, I did not have her get deeply involved in the economy, and she did not learn any of the crafting professions. Nor did I plan on having her reach the game's ceiling on experience points, somewhere north of 100, which would have taken months of effort, and she stopped at 50. A more important goal was to explore the entire territory of the continent depicted in *Perfect World*. One measure of this was how many of the locations she had reached that had teleport points, which allow instanta-neous travel to other teleport points that the avatar had already reached by other means, for payment of the virtual money used inside the game. Eventually Cleora had access to 60 such locations, distributed across the world. A less precise goal was to document at least one significant dimension of traditional Chinese culture.

The first step in most fantasy MMOs is to select a race for the charac-ter, which will determine how it appears, some of its powers, and where in the virtual world it begins its saga. I wanted Cleora to be very much herself, therefore Human and thus based in a town named Etherblade. Humans belong to one of two ability classes, blademasters or wizards, and since I could not imagine Cleora wielding a broadsword I made her a wizard. She arrived in China at the Inn of the Eagle, a tiny hotel on green grass amidst a few tall trees and a short distance from Etherblade. The local guide instructed her to kill ten ogre blossoms, huge animated flowers that seemed like carnivorous tulips, which got her to experience level 2, after which she killed a few pentastral beetles and swiftly reached level 3. Like most other popular MMOs, *Perfect World* starts the avatar in a safe tutorial area where the monsters do not spontaneously attack, are easy to kill, and earn experience levels very quickly.

Next, Cleora walked up the road to Etherblade, so-named because it is dominated by an immense sculpture of a sword blade thrust downward, as a tall as a skyscraper but having no function other than decoration. This is a rather fancy town in traditional Chinese architecture, with flawless and even monumental buildings having curved and sometimes multi-tiered roofs in pagoda style. The north side is protected by cliffs extending upward, while the other sides have walls constructed of gray stone blocks punctuated by gateways and occasionally decorated by dragon bas reliefs. A main thoroughfare runs through Etherblade. Nonplayer characters stand along it, and in side passages, assigning missions, offering virtual goods for sale, and performing other functions such as access to the bank where the avatar can store valuables. The

DOI: 10.1057/9781137490599.0007

center is a formal town hall, with the Elder (or mayor) at the entrance, managing the practical affairs of the community. Further back, near a grim statue of a tortoise with dragon features, stands the spiritual guide for human avatars, the Taoist Master. In meeting him, Cleora discovered the aspect of traditional Chinese culture she would need to learn about, Taoism.

Had she lived, the real Cleora would have accompanied her parents on an adventure to enter the Temple of Heaven in Beijing, where western-ers were forbidden to go back in 1879. Repulsed by guards whom they thought were willing to be bribed, but only if offered a princely sum, they explored and found a secret entrance part way in, then were accosted by guards again. At this point, her father left their group, and Cleora would have served as a kind of decoy, monopolizing the guards' atten-tion, as her father found a place where "with a little private engineering, the eighteen-feet wall could be scaled."[12] Although no bloodshed was involved, this incident was exactly like a mission in an MMO, and he used it again in the novel where Cleora was reborn, although sadly she did not take part in that particular adventure. Her father also used this as the introduction to his rather intellectual chapter on Chinese religion, implying that the amalgam of Taoism, Confucianism, and Buddhism was a hollow facade that a Christian missionary could penetrate, given sufficient intelligence and courage.

Cleora's father conceptualized Chinese religion as more primitive than Christianity, saturated with magical principles, of which he thought "fung-shway" (or feng shui) geomancy was fundamental. In his mind, this was the organizing principle that connected Taoism, Buddhism, and Confucianism, imposing the semblance of conceptual rigor upon a naturally incoherent collection of ancient superstitions. His description of Taoism was especially unsympathetic:

> Laou-tsze was the founder of Taouism, the polytheistic materialism of which represented the tendency to make a deity of or for every object of nature, to lower the whole religious system to a level of astrology and alchemy, and to degrade the priesthood and their followers into a sediment of ignorant quackery and conjury. Laou-tsze speculated upon the invisible powers in man and above man; he even took some steps toward important evangelical doctrine in his explanation of the principle of the "Taou," or "Wisdom," but the mastering spirit of his system was materialistic, polytheistic, and, next to Hinduism and Fetishism, the most grossly and debasingly idolatrous of any religious creed of the world.[13]

DOI: 10.1057/9781137490599.0007

Cleora was not forced to agree with her father in this severe criticism, and she looked forward to learning the truth about Taoism during her explorations of *Perfect World*. Her avatar was an adult, not a girl, so she already would have experienced the divorce of her parents, would have stayed with her brother and mother, and would have good reason to doubt his judgment.

In running an AVA, it can often be worthwhile not merely playing the role of the person inside the game, but outside as well. So, I took copies of James Legge's 1891 translation and Paul Carus's 1898 translation of Lao-Tse's book, *Tao-Teh-King*, to a local Chinese restaurant, to read as if through her eyes, selecting these editions because they would have been available to Cleora by age 30.[14] When I had read the book decades earlier for myself, it seemed very similar to Zen Buddhism or Existentialism, preaching mystical withdrawal from social life through what sometimes seemed a self-centered philosophy, and at other times seemed to deny the significance of the mind apart from nature.[15] But I had neither the erudition nor the experience of seeing how real people practiced Taoism, to put it in a proper social-scientific context. When I read the message in the fortune cookie I received near the end of the meal, it was difficult to be sure it was not a sentence from the book: "Now is the time to try something new." A day or two earlier, I had received a spam advertisement from the Cost Xpert software company, pretending to quote Lao-Tse: "Only he who knows his destination will find his way."

Carus translated Tao as *Reason*, but James Legge kept it as *Tao*, on the reasonable assumption that English did not already have a comparable concept. Despite having endured for 2,500 years in a society dominated by Confucianism, Taoism is often described as heterodox, or even as a sect or cult, but we cannot be sure how Lao-Tse himself intended it. Gilbert Reid commented, "His sayings are more of the nature of epigrams, and partake of the obscurity and mysticism of his whole religious philosophy. An epigram is often the exaggeration of a truth and for that reason Lao-tsze is not easily understood."[16] There are many other reasons why Lao-Tse is hard to understand, including the poetic nature of ancient, written Chinese. The social connections between Taoism and the practice of magic evolved over the centuries, as many other leaders contributed to the tradition.

I tend to think the reason that Taoism survived so long, in a society where Confucianism was integrated into the government and used as a test of quality in the elite, was that it served as an alternative but not an enemy. Being a Taoist can compensate some people for failing to belong to the elite, and its mystical statements about union with nature can support magical practices, but its main political doctrine is withdrawal rather than any kind of rebellion.[17] The creators of *Perfect World* have lived their entire lives in a culture where Maoism took the place of Confucianism, and we can imagine that for some real Chinese intellectuals today, Taoism might offer an alternative ideology, compatible with today's greater individualism, and yet not directly attacking the power structure. Perhaps, but this is all speculation. How does Taoism feature in *Perfect World*?

Taoist revivalism

The Taoist Master in Etherblade does not recite the words of Lao-Tse, but urges Cleora to work her way up a ladder of spiritual enlightenment and magical power to become a Celestial. Apparently, he represents a sect of Taoism often called the Way of the Celestial Masters, established centuries after Lao-Tse and described as the first really organized movement within Taoism.[18] Cleora had no desire to become a Celestial, but she saw that she would need to ascend at least a short distance up this spiritual ladder if she was to learn what it was all about. Taoism, like Chinese folk beliefs more generally, believed that each person possessed a life force called qi, and celestial masters needed to conserve their qi carefully. Both of these concepts map well onto standard practices in MMOs. An avatar ascends a ladder of power, over a period of weeks or months, and it might as well be conceptualized as spiritual advancement. At any given moment, an avatar posses some amount of "hit points" that allow it to be alive, and some degree of power, in the case of Cleora called health and mana, because these are standard Western terms.

So, Cleora needed to climb the experience ladder by completing missions for nonplayer characters, and some of these missions might also reveal Taoist principles. In exploring the virtual world, she would also find many temples and shrines, so she was very daring in penetrating all corners of the world, entering many areas where the monsters were far about her own power level, tagging the last of the 60 teleport locations when she was only level 20. Here are the teleport locations that could be reached directly from Teleport Master Yao, who stood just outside Etherblade:

Angler's Village: Very large town, houses on stilts near the ocean.

Archosaur: Huge city in traditional Chinese architectural style, dominated by colossal statues and mysterious platforms.

City of Raging Tides: Extravagant shapes, bright colors, grand thoroughfare; home of the Tideborn fish-human race.

City of the Lost: Rough stone building in a canyon, a huge temple with carved beasts; home of the Untamed beast-human race.

City of the Plume: Amid the roots of a huge, old, and very green tree; home of the Winged Elf race.

Elysium Village: Houses engulfed in flames, a dozen burned corpses lying in the street, all with name labels.

Hidden Heroes Village: Charming town between lakeside and hills.

Swiftwind Tribe: Totem poles, standing stones, canvas tents.

Tellus City: A lush formal garden, walled by four buildings, two with huge stone faces; home of the Earthguard race.

Timberfield: Lumbering community, many piles of huge logs.

Walled Stronghold: Elaborate fort with elevated walkways, turrets.

The 48 other locations to which Cleora could eventually teleport from Etherblade required stopping at intermediate destinations if her starting point was Etherblade, and asking the local teleport master for another instantaneous leap. The most magical place in the world, Heaven's Tear, could not be reached by walking or teleporting, but only by flying. Cleora could not get there until she had acquired a magic sword, which levitates in a horizontal position with her standing on the blade. At Heaven's Tear, three great boulders levitate in triangular formation, each supporting a pagoda with a five-level roof, and connected to a larger boulder at the center with a wide, circular platform. Standing at its edges, each near the center of a line between two pagodas, are three nonplayer characters who offered Cleora quests: the Celestial Elder, the Celestial Ancient, and the Celestial Recluse. At the very center of both triangles stands The Celestial One. The nearest levitation master is in The Silver Pool, where Cleora received several missions from the Psychic Master. But to get to the seer from the tear requires flying down past swarms of dangerous flying dragons. Here are ten other locations Cleora found fascinating, each in its own way:

City of a Thousand Streams: Immense mountaintop city, multiple pagodas, access to the Realm of Reflection where meditation gains experience.

City of Misfortune: Dramatic stone ruins on a small, distant island; Count Misfortune says life is like dust on the sea.

DOI: 10.1057/9781137490599.0007

Dreamweaver Port: A city beside the ocean, with a lighthouse, huge sailing ships, and a large population of NPCs.

Forgotten Sanctuary: Huge ruined temple framed by icy hills but decorated with flower baskets.

Immolation Camp: Dark, vault-like structures in an active lava field.

Nightfire Altar: Blazing electric focus in a strange crater, where the teleport master can be reached for escape only by difficult leaps or by flying.

Orchid Temple: Courtyard of modest but perfect red and gray buildings, presided over by Fang the Scholar.

Sanctuary: Two rows of formal buildings flanking a canal, bridged at two points, with eight small boats.

Shrine of the Ancestors: Ancient walled pond in a misty forest, with Seeker and Mystic NPCs.

Shrine of the Immortals: Mysterious yellow-gold hill-ringed structures, and a Reader of the Immortals NPC.

Many of the ordinary quests involve the meaning of death. As a non-player character (NPC) named Puhui the Taoist says, "Walking through time with a gentle grace, here I bow in reverence of our grand universe. Life, as we understand it, can last perhaps hundreds of years; but how can it possibly hope to share in eternity with Heaven?" Yet eternity after death seems more often to be horrible, and many missions involved putting a ghost to rest, whether peacefully or violently. For example, one long arc involves Ladywraith, a woman standing outside a monastery, who turns out to be both dead and dangerous. Eventually she tells her story, beginning with the deaths of her parents and her love for a man named Chang Liang:

> Wang Kuei was a villain in the village; a bully to everybody. He wanted to steal me from Chang Liang, so he killed him and tried to turn me into his concubine. I committed suicide to oppose him. I thought death would be my salvation, but after my death the Bloodraged Cadaver got me. The Bloodraged Cadaver was one of the most powerful ghosts, who existed over a thousand years ago. He used my desire for revenge and earned my trust. By the time I realized what his plot was, it was too late for me. I found out that he not only killed the villain but also everybody in the village. Sadly, by then I was completely under his control. He used me as bait to seduce those men and took their blood to strengthen his power.

So, by running Cleora across all the lands of *Perfect World*, I was myself completing a long quest arc to put a ghost to rest: the spirit of a little girl who died 12 times 12 years ago.

DOI: 10.1057/9781137490599.0007

Conclusion

The standard value system practiced by scholars of religion is based on tolerance, respecting believers no matter how alien their faith may be.[19] This seems all very admirable, except that it has two pernicious results. First, social scientific studies that identify harmful effects of religion, or that indicate that religious beliefs are false illusions, are not really welcome in this field. Second, despite often studying religious conflict, scholars cannot properly understand the valid functions conflict plays. An alternate theory holds that intense social movements are the real heart of any great religious tradition, and the moderate denominations are merely their decayed forms that have adapted to cosmopolitanism and secularization.[20] Sectarian movements often assert that only they possess the truth, while other religions are at best heresies, and some of them recruit very successfully by exploiting this claim of superiority, among powerless multitudes who suffer an inferiority complex. Once they become very successful, they tend to moderate, weaken, and make room for new sectarian movements. Superficially, the semi-secularized mainstream denominations appear to be the heart of the faith, but they are really superficial. Thus, Cleora's parents were only behaving in the normal religious manner when attacking Asian religions, preparing the way for her to do the same during her afterlife.

Notes

1 William Sims Bainbridge, "eIncarnations," *OUPblog*, April 12, 2013, http://blog. oup.com/2013/04/eincarnations-ancestor-veneration-avatars/.
2 William Sims Bainbridge, *eGods: Faith Versus Fantasy in Computer Gaming* (New York: Oxford University Press, 2013) p. 59.
3 Lucy Seaman Bainbridge, "One of the Pioneer Women in Medicine." *Medical Woman's Journal*, March 1921, 28(3); *Yesterdays* (New York: Fleming H. Revell, 1924) pp. 75–78.
4 William Folwell Bainbridge, *Self-Giving* (Boston: D. Lothrop, 1883), p. 262.
5 Lucy Seaman Bainbridge, *Round the World Letters* (Boston: Lothrop, 1882), p. 304.
6 Ibid., pp. 306–307.
7 http://tajmahal.gov.in/interior_decoration.html, accessed September 28, 2013.
8 Bainbridge, *Self-Giving*, p. 399.
9 Ibid., p. 402.

DOI: 10.1057/9781137490599.0007

10   Rodney Stark and William Sims Bainbridge, *A Theory of Religion* (New York: Toronto/Lang, 1987).

11   Stevan Harrell, "The Concept of Soul in Chinese Folk Religion." *The Journal of Asian Studies*, 1979, 38(3): 519–528.

12   William Folwell Bainbridge, *Around the World Tour of Christian Missions: A Universal Survey* (New York: Blackall, 1882), p. 169.

13   Ibid., p. 180.

14   James Legge, *The Texts of Taoism*, volume 39 in *The Sacred Books of China* (Oxford: Clarendon, 1891); Paul Carus, *Lao-Tze's Tao-Teh-King* (Chicago: Open Court, 1898); of course the author of the main text was Lao-Tse, but Legge and Carus did more than merely edit and translate, also adding commentaries.

15   Yu-Lan Fung, "Why China Has No Science: An Interpretation of the History and Consequences of Chinese Philosophy." *International Journal of Ethics*, 1922, 32(3): 237–263; Hwa Yol Jung, "Confucianism and Existentialism: Intersubjectivity as the Way of Man." *Philosophy and Phenomenological Research*, 1969, 30(2): 186–202.

16   Gilbert P. Reid, "Revolution as Taught by Taoism." *International Journal of Ethics*, 1925, 35(3): 289–295, p. 290.

17   King Shu Liu, "The Origin of Taoism." *The Monist*, 1917, 27(3): 376–389; Reid, "Revolution as Taught by Taoism," pp. 289–295; Shu-Ching Lee, "Intelligentsia of China." *American Journal of Sociology*, 1947, 52(6): 489–497.

18   Terry Kleeman, "Tianshi Dao," in *The Encyclopedia of Taoism*, edited by Fabrizio Pregadio (London: Routledge, 2008), pp. 981–986.

19   John Hinnells (ed.), *The Routledge Companion to the Study of Religion* (London: Routledge, 2010).

20   Rodney Stark and William Sims Bainbridge, *The Future of Religion* (Berkeley: University of California Press, 1985).

DOI: 10.1057/9781137490599.0007

6
Singing a Song (*EverQuest*)

Abstract: *This chapter celebrates joyful progress, to contrast with the gloom of the previous chapter, and it does so with musical metaphors. It also illustrates how living members of a family may use Internet to discover and share information about a long-deceased person, learning much about their ancestor that contributes to their lives in many ways, beyond merely enabling creation of an avatar based on him. The person on which the avatar was based was a poor boy who grew up in a small American town, learned to play the cornet, had a brief but successful career on the vaudeville circuit in the 1880s, then returned home to become a respected band leader, shopkeeper, and real estate investor. Thus, the sattva essence illustrates* progression, *advancement that is more than mere progress following one theme, but also involves modulation across themes and variations. The MMO is the original* EverQuest, *in which the avatar is a bard who learns to sing and play many songs, collecting musical instruments that confer magical powers, and eventually investing in real estate.*

Bainbridge, William Sims. *An Information Technology Surrogate for Religion: The Veneration of Deceased Family in Online Games.* New York: Palgrave MacMillan, 2014. DOI: 10.1057/9781137490599.0008.

> Progression: Advancement that is more than mere progress follow-
> ing one theme, but also involves modulation across themes and
> variations.

George Ernest Sims (1861–1936) will help us appreciate how learning
about a long-deceased person can illuminate the dynamics of a successful life's career, through revival inside *EverQuest*, a classical virtual world.
He was the father of my grandfather Sims, but very little information
about him was directly transmitted to me. His case illustrates the potential for Family Renaissance, as email communication with my two "Sims
cousins," Barbara Houston and Stephen Rohn, stimulated our discovery
of considerable information about him in online newspaper archives.
His career was that of a "music man" who became a real estate investor,
thus suggesting the metaphor that life is a song, ideally with a coherent
theme, some degree of melodic modulation, and a coda at the end.

Looking backward

We usually define immortality as what happens after death, perhaps
as an afterlife. But it also can be conceptualized in terms of what
happens before death, as each positive event connects to the ones
that occurred before. Conventional notions of immortality imply an
infinite life, yet we did not exist before we were conceived, and there is
something unbalanced about having a beginning but no end. An alternate conception of perfection is integrity, more logical and less greedy
than immortality. Musical compositions, after all, are finite, yet some
approach perfection. No one sings a song forever, yet perhaps a person
may become a song.

When my grandfather William E. Sims died in 1959, my mother had
to arrange transfer of his body to Evergreen Cemetery in Canton, New
York, where her mother had already been interred. She found that there
were two funeral homes in that area, and selected one simply because the
other had an Irish name and she assumed it was Roman Catholic. Only
then did she discover that the rejected funeral home was actually in the
house that formerly belonged to her grandfather. My sister and I rode
with her to Canton, and we passed the house, which was quite impressive. Recently, I searched the Web for the funeral home, and learned that
it had belonged to O'Leary Funeral Service since the 1930s and was at

DOI: 10.1057/9781137490599.0008

32 Park Street. Despite the fact that the business had moved out in 2011, its website displayed a fine photograph of this exceedingly ornate home, complete with a turret.

Houses are expressions of their owners, as well as being environments that shape the lives of their residents. According to the Zillow online service, the house has three bedrooms and three baths, was built in 1930, and sold in 2011 for about $200,000. Canton is not an expensive place to live, and the Connecticut home of my parents mentioned in the three concluding chapters, fire damaged in the 1960s but completely repaired, is now listed as worth ten times as much. But for its area, the Sims home in Canton was substantial and even fancy. However, immediately after my great-grandfather's death, his widow placed a classified advertisement in the local newspaper offering rooms for rent, an indication that she was not exactly rich, at that point during the Great Depression. These facts suggest that absolutely astonishing amounts of detailed information about some deceased persons and their environments are beginning to be available over Internet.

While communicating with Barbara and Stephen about our family origins, I naturally searched for information related to our grandfather, William E. Sims. I knew he was especially proud of one mission he had done as an attorney, acting a little like an action fantasy hero, because it involved intellectual combat against the Soviet Union. I was excited to discover that he had written up the full story. The front page of the *St. Lawrence Plaindealer* newspaper for September 17, 1929, proclaimed: "Former Canton Boy Wins $5,000,000 Suit: Attorney W. E. Sims Figures in Interesting Case, Defeats Attempt of Russian Soviet to Secure Church Property in United States." According to the Bureau of Labor Statistics, $5,000,000 in 1929 would be $70,000,000 in 2014, but really the case was more significant than that. Prior to his involvement, the Soviet Union had won a judgment giving it control over the properties of the Russian Orthodox Church in America, but my grandfather successfully had this overturned on appeal, a crucial step in assuring that an independent Russian church would survive, even if Marxist atheism did triumph in its home land.

This story was published because our grandfather told it to his father, when visiting the old family home, and George E. Sims had close connections with the newspaper staff. When I shared this article with Barbara, she picked up on the fact that it mentioned his father, and was able to find the older man's exceedingly detailed obituary on the front

DOI: 10.1057/9781137490599.0008

page of the March 10, 1936 issue of Canton's *Commercial Advertiser*. One detail that helped us find over a dozen other references was that his name was often given as G. Ernest Sims, rather than George E. Sims, and that his friends called him Ernie. I quickly saw that he should be the subject of one chapter of this book, and that his avatar's name should be Gernest.

Ernie was born on September 3, 1861, and the obituary told us that his father, William, died when he was quite young. Going online I found a picture of William's tombstone, learning that he died on October 8, 1866 at the age of 37, thus soon after Ernie's fifth birthday. His mother, Jane, subsequently married the county sheriff, William Tanner, but she was buried with her first husband, sharing the tombstone of William Sims, when she died in 1894. Ernie was a very industrious child, and earned money using a printing press he had acquired. The obituary mentions that his brother, Charles, worked at the local newspaper, and a lifelong connection to the local print media may partially explain why so much was published about Ernie after his death. But the obituary is very clear that in those days before radio and when even the phonograph was just being invented, one of the socially most significant media was musical performance:

> The youth in his early teens had a desire to learn to play band instruments. Those were the days when the brass band was found in every community, and marching bands, sometimes two or three of them were at Fourth of July celebration, County Fair, fireman's tournament. He was able to secure a cornet from money earned and he proved an apt pupil. At the age of fourteen or fifteen he was playing with the Canton Fireman's Band. The old band men of those days, now all gone, were struck with wonder by the ability the Sims boy showed in blowing a horn. One day a minstrel show came to Canton and the boy met a talented cornetist who could triple tongue his horn. "Show me how you do it," appealed the Sims boy, and before the company left Canton the following day the boy was able to triple tongue with his instructor.

At the age of 16, Ernest became a band leader and music teacher. At 19 he joined the Oakes Brothers Concert Company and became a headliner in what was emerging as the Midwest vaudeville circuit, billed as "the wonder boy cornetist." My cousin Stephen scanned in and shared with me and his sister two photos of Ernie at this point in his career. One is a close-up of him smoking a cheroot, wearing a brimmed hat, and grinning wickedly into the camera. In the other, he stands on a vaudeville stage with a colleague, both holding cheroots and pretending to

DOI: 10.1057/9781137490599.0008

be relaxed. A long reminiscence of Ernie, published on page 7 of the *Commercial Advertiser*, April 22, 1947, explained the difficult conditions of his childhood, which shaped his aggressive character:

> Sims, the boy, had to struggle for a livelihood. He made candy and peddled it on a board with a strap around his neck, and the board held horizontally across his chest. His mother, a second time a widow, the Widow Jane Tanner, was a woman of parts. She saved and saved and gathered together her savings and invested it in real estate until she owned many homes in the village. She ran a millinery store in the little cottage that stood just east of the Advertiser block of today. And in the eighties the little store or millinery shop housed the organ, piano and musical instruments and supplies of her son, Ernie, as he was called in those years.

The same article reports a financial dispute Ernie had later in life with a local bank in which he had invested, and legal records dating from 1914 reveal that his son served as his attorney in a court battle they won against a utility company in Colorado in which Ernie had invested. After leaving the vaudeville circuit, Ernie had taken over his mother's store, becoming the local agent selling pianos and other musical instruments, and expanding her real estate investments. As a very successful head of bands in the area, he used the music business as public relations for sale of most everything else available in the town.

His was not an easy life, as indicated by the fact that he was married three times. His first wife, Carrie Finnimore (1863–1923), was a local girl, and my grandfather was their only child. When she died, Ernie married a second Carrie, who had been married twice before and had been a Judson, a Welch and an Adams before becoming a Sims. She was Carrie Esther Adams of Cambridge Massachusetts, the mother of Mildred Welch (1889–1952), who had married Ernie's son William. My mother used to joke with her sister Audrey, the mother of Barbara and Stephen, that they were not really sisters but cousins. I do not know how common this kind of familial consolidation used to occur, in which the survivors of two marriages connected by the marriage of their children themselves marry, but it happened once on the Bainbridge side of my family as well, and historical demographers report that family life in earlier centuries was less stable than we like to imagine.[1]

Ernie's third marriage came the year after the second Carrie's death in 1933, to Maude Revell, when he was already 72 years old. Her first husband had been run over by a train in 1925. It is noteworthy that Ernie's son did not attend the wedding, and that Maude had agreed

DOI: 10.1057/9781137490599.0008

to a prenuptial agreement limiting her rights of inheritance, chiefly to their home in Canton. At his death, Ernie owned $127,268 in stock and bonds, which the Bureau of Labor Statistics suggests might be worth about $1,774,000 in terms of 2014 money, much of which was inherited by my grandfather, and some of that was passed down all the way to me. My thanks to the great-grandfather I never personally knew are a rather different form of immortality from that provided by religion. Another suggestive tiny detail of his history was the fact that his third wedding was not presided over by an ordinary clergyman, but by Ernie's friend, Dr. Richard Eddy Sykes, who held a doctor of divinity degree but belonged to the slightly unconventional Universalist denomination, primarily was known for being president of St. Lawrence University in Canton, and had been Ernie's boyhood friend.

Music is an alternate reality, and philosopher Schopenhauer even argued that the entire world is *embodied music*, as humans experience it.[2] Influenced by him, Richard Wagner and Friedrich Nietzsche both suggested that music could unify culture.[3] More recently, Leonard B. Meyer compared theories of music that considered it to be the most pure form of emotional expression, versus an abstract description of the surrounding world, versus a cognitive map of the ways a human mind processes information.[4] Perhaps a fourth possibility, that unites the others, is that music is a form of action, seeing it from the perspective of the performer rather than the audience. One remarkable action in Ernie's life, that connects music to religion and both of them to mortality, is the fact that he donated an organ to the county jail. Perhaps the music played on it inspired the prisoners to transform their lives, more than did the words of the hymns.

A daunting tutorial

Three criteria determined which virtual world would become Gernest's main home. First, it needed to be one where a very successful career based in music would be possible. Second, it needed to be one I had not already explored, which at this point in my research narrowed the choices considerably. Third, I felt it must permit discovery of an excellent past, parallel to our discoveries about the real past life of G. Ernest Sims. The best choice was the original *EverQuest*, which launched in 1999 but was still very active, adding its 20th expansion during the time of my research. Gernest could be a bard, a music-oriented class that sings songs having magical powers, some of which are enabled or increased by a musical instrument.[5]

The play choices and user interface of *EverQuest* are so complex as to be daunting, as every few months for 14 years more and more had been added, and little removed. One thing that did not come with the game, when I downloaded it, was a general instruction manual. I frequently consulted the online player forums, finding them sometimes helpful but often poorly informed and outdated. The game itself offered a complex tutorial area, where Gernest stayed as long as he could, leaving only at level 9.

From the standpoint of story, the tutorial zone is a subterranean slave labor camp, the Mines of Gloomingdeep, currently controlled by Kobolds who have enslaved Goblins. A slave revolt has broken out in the Mines of Gloomingdeep, involving NPCs belonging to many races and classes, some of whom serve as tutors to teach new players how to operate their avatars, on their way toward escaping the mines. The action began with killing cave bats and cave rats, learning how to wield a sword and loot their corpses of any resources they might carry. During combat, the main text chat window filled with statements reporting the actions both Gernest and the bat had taken. Each step was the equivalent of a dice roll in *Dungeons and Dragons*, in which a combination of chance and a set of interaction rules determined what would happen. Here, for the example, is the beginning of one of Gernest's first battles:

> A cave bat flies forward, gnashing its teeth.
> You slash a cave bat for 8 points of damage.
> A cave bat tries to bite YOU, but misses!
> You slash a cave bat for 8 points of damage.
> A cave bat tries to bite YOU but misses!
> You try to slash a cave bat, but miss!
> A cave bat bites you for 6 points of damage.
> You try to slash a cave bat, but miss!
> A cave bat bites you for 1 point of damage.
> ....
> You slash a cave bat for 5 points of damage.
> You have slain a cave bat.

During this combat, Gernest was singing a magical song that gave him greater fortitude, "Chant of Battle." Early in the tutorial, Gernest had interacted with a nonplayer character named Rytan who instructed him on how to scribe a song into his spellbook and put an icon on an action bar so he could sing it.

Each of the many missions assigned by a tutor would show up in Gernest's quest journals, including learning about weapons, armor, hotbars, communication, and two very useful interface tools, "find path" and maps. Under appropriate circumstances, such as seeking a particular quest giver when the search itself was not part of the puzzle, the "find path" command would produce a fluctuating path of light Gernest could follow to his selected destination. Pressing the M key would bring up an outline map of the tunnels of Gloomingdeep or whatever zone he happened to be in. Much later, after Gernest had escaped, he entered zones where the maps did not work, which required me to learn more about them. Each map was stored in the form of a text file, consisting of a series of coordinates, which the game's map interface would interpret to produce a chart in the form of simple outlines of areas and occasional labels. Here, for example, are the last lines of the file tutorialb.txt that labels 8 points on the Gloomingdeep map:

P 342.5933, −703.0335, −22.2596, 127, 0, 0, 3, Gloomingdeep_Jail
P 423.5385, 838.2468, −48.4979, 127, 0, 0, 3, Gloomfang_Lair
P 943.1806, 458.2474, −181.7635, 127, 0, 0, 3, Dig_Site_One
P 1801.7162, 253.9825, −106.3666, 127, 0, 0, 3, Fort_Gloomingdeep
P 909.9113, 0.2970, −30.4056, 127, 0, 0, 3, Dig_Site_Two
P 55.8279, 188.8215, 12.1597, 127, 0, 0, 3, Mushrooms
P 129.5970, 14.7314, 15.3202, 0, 240, 0, 3, Slave_Revolt_Camp
P 175.4439, −137.9834, 14.2116, 127, 0, 0, 3, Escape_Tunnel_(Exit)

Any industrious player could create such maps and share them with other players. Indeed, most of the maps of advanced zones distributed with the *EverQuest* software had apparently been created by players. When some maps stopped working, I checked their files and discovered that they were empty, and no replacement seemed to be available from the main *EverQuest* website. Googling "everquest maps" located a website named MapFiend, from which a fuller set of player-created maps could be downloaded, and replacing the defective files from this source solved the problem nicely.

Perhaps the most important step in the tutorial was learning how to hire a mercenary. This is an assistant secondary avatar that cannot be controlled in fine detail, but adds strength to one or another aspect of the main avatar. Bards are a melee class, who stand toe-to-toe with the enemy. For much of his career in *EverQuest*, Gernest held a mace in his right hand, and a short sword in his left hand, bashing and slashing. It seemed logical to select a mercenary who would be a healer, restoring Gernest's health as wounds depleted it. The two healers of different power levels Gernest hired during his career, Bearini and Pukjini, were both women, and healer avatars tend to be female in MMOs.

To beat the band

EverQuest proved to be a good environment for reviving several aspects of the life of G. Ernest Sims, but not all and not perfectly. For one thing, bards did not form bands with other bards to play music together, something minstrels in *Lord of the Rings* can do, as we shall see in the final chapter. Rather, the music of one bard could assist avatars of other kinds, and MMO teams are rather emphatically based on division of labor across very different specializations. He was able to experiment with sharing his musical abilities, however, because his hired NPC mercenary counted as a member of his team.

For example, at early levels while battling enemies, Bearini would stand a short distance from the fight, as Gernest battled the foe toe-to-toe, and she would cast healing spells to restore his health whenever it got low. At very early experience levels he would sing "Chant of Battle," and protective musical notes would begin to fly around both Bearini and himself. The in-game description of this level 1 song called it a "simple tune that increases the strength, dexterity, and armor class of group members." Later on, however, he found that both Bearini and Pukjini could heal themselves if they were injured, so he would sing songs that increased his own attack power, such as "Jonthan's Whistling Warsong" (level 7: "An ancient war song that speeds your attacks and raises your armor class and strength") and "Jonthan's Provocation" (level 45: "An ancient war song that increases your attack speed, strength, and attack rating.").

When he reached level 50 of general experience, Gernest had learned fully 63 different songs, many of which required or would be enhanced by the use of a musical instrument. For example, "Chant of Battle" used percussion, and Gernest's collection of instruments included a hand drum. The rest of his basic collection consisted of a horn, a wooden flute, a mandolin, and a lute. He also had Sarialiyn's Lute, which was really a quest item rather than a functioning musical instrument, and an advanced brass instrument, McVaxius' Horn of War. In his training,

DOI: 10.1057/9781137490599.0008

he had reached Master level in both singing and brass instruments, the latter enacting the cornet expertise of G. Ernest Sims.

He had to be careful with some of the spells, because they might affect friendly nearby NPCs in an adverse way. For example, upon reaching level 50 in celebration he sang "Chords of Dissonance" while playing a stringed instrument inside friendly Crescent Reach city—"clashing notes that cause between 14 and 27 damage and lower the armor class of any nearby creature"—inadvertently hurting two NPC wardens who immediately killed him, thereby driving his experience back below 50 when he resurrected!

The motto of the Sims department store, "everything from pins to pianos," can be interpreted in many ways. When Gernest was in action, he followed the maxim that every piece of available loot was valuable, a pin as well as a piano—although he never actually found a piano in *EverQuest*—and he would always loot corpses that other players had failed to loot after a kill. Another way to interpret his motto is as a model for his career that built from his childhood interest in music to commerce and real estate investment, in a series of steps. That inspired Gernest to use a phased approach to exploration, staying in each of a small number of areas until he had exhausted its potential, and only then moving on to an area at a higher level that also was suitable for a long stay.

For example, there was an area just north of a camp of NPC merchants and quest-givers in Blightfire Moors where he invested several experience levels killing giant animated mushrooms, beating Dragoneater their boss dozens of times, to loot very valuable items from him repeatedly. The crucial point of selecting this area was its proximity to the merchants and quest givers, and the fact that other monsters were not constantly wandering through the area, which made some other places rather undesirable. Also, the entrance to the Goru`kar Mesa zone was a short run north, so Gernest could quickly escape if he got attacked by several giant mushrooms at once, as they could not follow him there.

Although this strategy was a form of solo play, Gernest did very quickly join a very nice guild, called Have Heart, which was led by a married couple in which the husband's main avatar was Torrential, and the wife's was Lenani. But they and other central members were much higher level than Gernest, so he could not join their primary team missions. Indeed, the main function of the guild for Gernest was helping him "have heart," that is being more confident and enthusiastic, and learning how best

DOI: 10.1057/9781137490599.0008

to meet the challenges of the game. Every five levels in his ascent up the experience ladder, Gernest would receive hearty congratulations through the guild's text chat, because it automatically sent the news of his accomplishment. Similarly, whenever a new member would join the guild, he would say "welcome," and when an achievement message was broadcast concerning another member, he expressed congratulations with the colloquial, "Gratz!"

Thus, much of the social life of Have Heart was conducted remotely, not only because the people operating the avatars lived at different geographic locations, but because the avatars themselves were seldom in the same zone of *EverQuest*. Gernest did occasionally encounter a fellow member, and in the game an avatar's name and the name of the guild were displayed over their heads. Also, Have Heart possessed a Guild Hall and eventually a Palatial Guild Hall and a neighborhood where individual members could set up houses.

Have Heart opened its residential neighborhood during the period when Gernest was a member, and as soon as he could afford to, he rented a plot and placed a one-room house upon it. Darrque had a small house at 105 Guild Way, set in a nice yard with trees and various outdoor decorations, so Gernest took the plot right across the entrance road to the Guild Hall, at 104 Guild Way. Rather than following Darrque's tasteful style, Gernest furnished his home as a fun house, filled by his large collection of *plushies*, life-size animated dolls of mostly humanoid monsters. I felt this harmonized with the vaudeville period of Ernie's life, in the 1880s. Later, Gernest rented both 104 and 105 Guild Way, flanking the driveway of the Palatial Guild Hall, and symbolizing Ernie's expansive real estate business.

Duplicating Ernie's success as a merchant proved too difficult for me to accomplish in *EverQuest*. From time to time as he ascended the 50 levels of experience I was willing to climb, he visited The Bazaar where avatars bought and sold goods they had collected or crafted. Eventually, he tried his hand at selling, which required buying a satchel in which to place goods, and he filled with odd items he had looted during his travels. The procedure was then to stand on a low platform in one of several halls, offering his wares for sale. MMOs other than *EverQuest* do not require avatars to be in the market when they sell, and I could spare Gernest this indignity by purchasing the most recent game expansion, in addition to the monthly subscription I already paid. Given that his explorations were near an end, I did not do so.

DOI: 10.1057/9781137490599.0008

Conclusion

After running Gernest for 195 hours in *EverQuest*, it seemed time for him to take a vacation. I have two photographs of him taken late in life, visiting Egypt, so I briefly sent a Gernest avatar on a tour on Ancient Egypt in the noncombat MMO, *A Tale in the Desert*. That was the coda of the first movement of a Sims symphony, and the second movement would be a duet, played by his son and daughter-in-law who technically was also his step-daughter, in an MMO that belonged to a later generation of computer games. I really do believe that social scientists should consider developing rigorous models of human behavior, based on the rather well-developed concepts, categories, and even notation of music. This is not the place for such a symphony, in which the roles of multiple players weave polyphony, and a book is not a cantata. Yet while exploring the most modern artistic medium, massively multiplayer online games, we can contemplate the possibilities for future social science offered by more traditional media.

Notes

1   Peter Laslett, *The World We Have Lost* (London: Methuen, 1965).
2   Arthur Schopenhauer, *The World as Will and Idea* (London: Trübner, 1883–1886).
3   Richard Wagner, *The Art-Work of the Future* (Lincoln: University of Nebraska Press, 1993); Friedrich Wilhelm Nietzsche, *The Birth of Tragedy and the Case of Wagner* (New York: Vintage, 1967).
4   Leonard B. Meyer, *Emotion and Meaning in Music* (Chicago: University of Chicago Press, 1956); *Music, the Arts, and Ideas* (Chicago: University of Chicago Press, 1994).
5   Sony Online Entertainment, *EverQuest Role-Playing Game: Player's Handbook* (Stone Mountain, GA: White Wolf, 2002), pp. 53–55, 185–199.

DOI: 10.1057/9781137490599.0008

7

Uniting a Couple (*Guild Wars 2*)

Abstract: *Other chapters emphasize this triad relationship: avatar–sattva–user. This chapter introduces the possibility of a fourth element, another person whose relationship with the deceased person shapes the character of the avatar. Indeed, this chapter will diverge from the pattern of one avatar per chapter, and use a pair of avatars representing both members of a married couple. The husband was the son of the person memorialized in the previous chapter, and the wife was both his daughter-in-law and step-daughter, so one of the best new MMOs, was selected, Guild Wars 2, a cultural descendant of EverQuest. In future, living family members may explore an MMO together, each playing the role of a different deceased relative, but this chapter follows the simpler approach of having one user alternate between the avatars, but having them interact extensively with each other. Either approach requires partnership, operation of two or more related avatars inside the same virtual world, cooperating with each other. Each member of the couple was represented by a different class of avatar. She was a plant person, symbolizing the husband's love of horticulture, and he was a craftsman, manufacturing virtual goods from the resources she shared with him from her adventures.*

Bainbridge, William Sims. *An Information Technology Surrogate for Religion: The Veneration of Deceased Family in Online Games.* New York: Palgrave MacMillan, 2014.
DOI: 10.1057/9781137490599.0009

> Partnership: Operation of two or more related avatars inside the
> same virtual world, cooperating with each other.

Other chapters emphasize this triad relationship: avatar–sattva–user. This
chapter introduces the possibility of a fourth element, another person
whose relationship with the deceased person shapes the character of the
avatar. Indeed, this chapter will diverge from the pattern of one avatar
per chapter, and use a pair of avatars representing both members of a
married couple, my maternal grandparents, Mildred Elizabeth Judson
Welch Adams Sims (1889–1952) and William E. Sims (1886–1959),
mentioned in the previous chapter. Note that he outlived her by about
seven years, so I felt it was important to be reunited in a virtual world
that was of very high quality and offered a way in which they could
cooperate, while representing very different kinds of avatar and action.
The choice was *Guild Wars 2*, a high-quality and popular modern fantasy
gameworld.

A flowering romance

I remember very fondly but also vaguely Mildred, my maternal grandmother. Thus, this chapter will have some of the same challenge as the
ones about Ernest and Cleora, filling in the blanks to the extent that
is practical and congruent with the personal goals of the role-player. I
recall her having a calm but clear voice, with a New England accent, but
I do not recall anything she said. From the photographs and artifacts
that survived her, I know she was physically very fit. For years our attic
preserved her white figure skates, and my mother said she was expert
in their use. She must have suffered from allergies, because I recall my
mother blaming our New York allergist for failing to report early signs of
her cancer, because he felt oncology was not his specialty.

My mother spoke of her mother as an "orphan," and research through
paper documents and online searches clarified what she meant by this
term. On May 25, 1939, Mildred completed the complex genealogical
form for membership in the Daughters of the American Revolution,
as a direct descendent of James Frye: "Colonel of regiment of militia in
Revolution. Wounded in Battle of Charlestown Heights June 16, 1775, and
died from the effect of wounds six months later." This affidavit said that
Mildred herself was born March 21, 1889 in Cambridge, Massachusetts,

DOI: 10.1057/9781137490599.0009

descended from Frye through her father, Wilfred M. Welch, who had been born in Cambridge on April 27, 1864 and died on November 7, 1897. That implies that Mildred was only eight years old when her father died, and that is the sense in which she was an orphan. Her mother, Carrie Esther Judson, was born on August 1, 1870, and did not die until March 27, 1933.

The story of Mildred's childhood is more complex than those simple dates might suggest, and searching online provided only partial clarity. Carrie Esther Judson was married three times, beginning with Wilfred Welch. On September 7, 1895, the local newspaper, *The Cambridge Chronicle*, reported on page 4: "Mr George B. Adams, son of Mr and Mrs John P. Adams, of No 10 Shepard street, and Mrs Carrie Judson Welch were married on Thursday evening at the home of the bride's mother, Mrs W. A. Judson, No 73 Magazine street, by Rev Charles Olmstead. It was a quiet home wedding, only relatives being present." The newspaper did not admit that the wedding was held at home because Carrie must have divorced Wilfred, given that he had in fact not died yet and divorcee weddings tended then not to be celebrated in church. A genealogy book confirms Wilfred's death date, although of course Mildred must have known her father outlived his marriage to her mother.[1]

Aside from a list on the first page of the May 24, 1890 issue of *The Cambridge Chronicle*, reporting that Wilfred served as a census enumerator that year, we have found little information about him online. We have formal photographs of him made in the studios of two different Boston photographers, both showing an apparently serious, well-dressed young man wearing eyeglasses, one matching a rather beautiful picture presumed to be of Carrie. Among the early pictures we have of Mildred is one showing her in good attire riding a huge if spindly tricycle, of uncertain age but perhaps ten and thus well after her mother married Adams. His obituary, published on page 5 of the March 8, 1913 issue of *The Cambridge Tribune* noted that he worked for the local electric utility, saying: "His natural aptitude for figures made him a valuable accountant, and he was entrusted with work involving a large amount of detail and systematizing. Although of a retiring, undemonstrative disposition, Mr. Adams's intimate friends knew him for a man of the strictest integrity and loyalty." This obituary also reported that he was a charter member and the secretary of the New England Skating Association, and thus the source of Mildred's own skating hobby. The obituary describes her as his "step-daughter."

DOI: 10.1057/9781137490599.0009

The previous chapter already introduced William E. Sims, so only a little more is needed here. He was a brilliant intellectual who earned his law degree from Harvard, which must be when he met Mildred, since Harvard was in her home town. For much of his career he was a partner in the Wall Street law firm that bore his name even for decades after his death: Sage, Gray, Todd, and Sims. When it finally dissolved in 1987, it was on the 100th floor of the World Trade Center, an address that vanished violently on September 11, 2001.[2] He was an avid reader of both factual history and murder mysteries, but his most active late-life hobby was gardening, which celebrates life, so the central metaphor of this chapter will be considering Mildred to have been his most beautiful flower.

At his retirement from the practice of law in 1951, he wrote a memo about one of his most perplexing clients, so that the attorneys who took over the work would have the necessary background. I recall him pointing to the desk not far from his favorite chair in his library, and mentioning the memo. Six decades later, realizing I had a damaged but still legible copy, I decided to figure out why he had thought it was worth remembering. The first page was missing, but I was able to determine that it was a history of a sugar company called USCOS, founded by Benjamin F. Johnston, who had explored business opportunities in Mexico. The memo says: "He found, near Los Mochis, a broken-down and bankrupt socialistic experiment in communal sugar raising and manufacture, which he took over and, after various vicissitudes, including one receivership, finally got the company on a stable footing and, with occasional bad years, it has fairly well prospered ever since." The full story of this radical commune,[3] plus the aggressive corporation that followed it and somehow prospered during the Mexican civil war, is so remarkable that it would be worthy of its own MMO game!

Second blossoming

Thinking of the seven years in which William E. Sims outlived Mildred, I first revived both of them in the high-quality MMO, *Rift*, assigning each to a different one of the two diametrically opposed factions, as a metaphor for their separation by death.[4] She was represented by an avatar named Mildryth in the religiously devout Guardian faction, and he was represented by Eilliam in the scientific and anti-religious Defiant faction.

DOI: 10.1057/9781137490599.0009

This was not intended to suggest that the two sattvas were opposed in their orientation to religion, but as the most effective way to separate them conceptually within the *Rift* world. Indeed, separation versus unification is a key concept of that MMO, especially the dichotomy between the natural world and supernatural forces that sought to invade it through rifts in the barrier that prevented chaos from dissolving the natural order.

When I began research inside *Guild Wars 2* on June 7, 2013, I had already studied the original *Guild Wars*, and had a general sense of the mythos, although the two MMOs are very different in technical design. I had only a vague sense of the kind of avatar I wanted to begin with, a female among the sylvan plant people, described thus in the character selection part of the game interface: "Sylvari are not born. They awaken beneath the Pale Tree with knowledge gained in their pre-life Dream. These noble beings travel, seeking adventure and pursuing quests. They struggle to balance curiosity with duty, eagerness with chivalry, and warfare with honor. Magic and mystery entwine to shape the future of this race that has so recently appeared." The recent appearance of the Sylvari in the mythos, compared with the long histories of other races, stems from the fact they did not exist in the past. Rather, the Pale Tree, often called the Mother Tree, sprouted in a human graveyard from a magic seed. Thus, in a sense, Sylvari are hybrids of plants and humans, a collective re-blossoming of humanity.

I named my Sylvari avatar Vanilla Bailiwick, terms that hearkened back to my early childhood. Vanilla was my favorite ice cream, and "Bailiwick" was the name my mother assigned to the New England "saltbox" home built in 1743 we lived in, on farmland near Bethel, Connecticut, a name partly derived from the fact it had once been owned by P. T. Barnum's partner in the circus business, James Anthony Bailey. Only as I played Vanilla did I begin to sense she represented a person from my childhood, namely my mother's mother. If she was the main genetic path from which descendants like me inherited hay fever, then reviving her as a flower suggests that allergies should be incorporated in the metaphor.

When Vanilla reached level 20 of experience, I created a second avatar, a member of the stern Norn race, named explicitly William E. Sims. Remembering how he struggled for over five years against the gruesome cancer that finally killed him, I selected the necromancer class, intimately connected with death. But reading the description on the class selection screen, I noted, "Necromancers draw life force and use it to strengthen

DOI: 10.1057/9781137490599.0009

or heal themselves and others." Although he had been an historian and attorney, he was also a fan of science fiction—or *friction* as he preferred to call it. He boasted that his massive stone home in Monroe, New York, was the oldest building in the county that used steel in its construction, although this referred merely to the fact that the lintel over the back door was a section of railway track. One of the home movies he made, which we still possess in digital form, shows no human beings, but the complex workings of farm machinery. Thus, I felt it was entirely appropriate to have his avatar emphasize technical skills.

Having William E. Sims enter *Guild Wars 2* long after his wife did seemed appropriately symbolic of the fact that she died first, thus earlier entering whatever afterlife may exist. His entry actually gave more meaning to the name Vanilla, representing the purity he saw in his wife. Also, vanilla is a member of the orchid family, and in his greenhouse he especially raised orchids. After the earliest levels of the game's tutorial, I decided not to have his avatar do any adventure quests at all, but rather experience them vicariously through Vanilla, just as he experienced history through reading books. To connect them, rather than separate them as I had done in *Rift*, I had him emphasize all the crafting skills, using raw materials she would gather from the environment and place in their joint bank account, which could be accessed in any of the game's cities. At the time, the experience level cap was 80, and when she reached it the materials she had sent him allowed him to reach level 34, because in GW2 crafting confers regular experience.

Vanilla even looked a bit like Mildred Sims, but covered with tiny elegant leaves, like a plant. Her class was elementalist, the closest to nature, which meant that she could operate secondary avatars based on one of the four elements. She mostly used fire, precisely because it was the most frightening for plants like herself, switched to water on those rare occasions when an enemy was resistant to fire, and did not rely upon air or earth. While Vanilla was still dreaming, a ghostly woman named Caithe spoke to her, warning that something was poisoning the Dream, in the form of a dragon, and arranging to meet as soon as Vanilla awoke. Within the dream a white stag offered freedom, thereby connecting a plant woman to a member of the animal kingdom.

With only modest distortion, one could imagine that Vanilla was not only Mildred but also Eve from the Bible, still living partially within the Garden of Eden. The official *Guild Wars 2* wiki says this about Sylvari religion: "The sylvari have an agnostic view of the Human Gods, wishing

DOI: 10.1057/9781137490599.0009

to see proof of the gods' existence and work. They venerate the Ventari Tablet as their most sacred artifact and testament. The Pale Tree is also much revered, though more as a wise parent than as a deity. If the sylvari need counseling, they often travel to the heart of the mighty tree and commune with her there."[5] This metaphor becomes serious theory, in the light of *The Raw and the Cooked*, by structuralist anthropologist Claude Lévi-Strauss.[6] Many cultures have a myth about how humanity came to be separated from nature, expulsion from the Garden of Eden being the most familiar.

Vanilla, however, was only partially separated from nature, and union with William E. Sims would require her first to gain a degree of independence. Whether this would be a struggle was not clear at first, because for Sylvari in general, a search for greater individuality was considered appropriate. The Ventari Tablet described in the quotation about their religion, lists seven sacred principles:

I. Live life well and fully, and waste nothing.
II. Do not fear difficulty. Hard ground makes stronger roots.
III. The only lasting peace is the peace within your own soul.
IV. All things have a right to grow. The blossom is brother to the weed.
V. Never leave a wrong to ripen into evil or sorrow.
VI. Act with wisdom, but act.
VII. From the smallest blade of grass to the largest mountain, where life goes—so, too, should you.[7]

For her first seven levels of experience, Vanilla gained familiarity with the environment in Caledon Forest, fighting insects, learning to love dogs as Mildred actually did, and developing proper relations of conflict or friendship with many kinds of creatures. Then a vision came to her, Prayer of Protection, in which she again saw the white stag. She met Caithe, a Valiant of the Pale Tree who belonged to the Cycle of Night, one of four divisions of Sylvari society, defined by when during the day she was born: Dawn, Noon, Dusk, or Night. This was the cycle in which Vanilla herself was born, and has this motto: "We make our own decisions, and we come and go as we please, nimble of mind and body."

Caithe introduced Vanilla to Malomedies, leader of the Cycle of Night who has some ability to predict the future. He urges her to stalk the stag, but be cautious, because the Dream does not perfectly reflect the world of nature. Indeed, the stag represents hope, and if it is perverted, hope

DOI: 10.1057/9781137490599.0009

can cause despair and hatred. In her search, she is assisted by a Sylvari man named Gavin, who only at the end reveals that he is a member of the Nightmare Court cult that rejects the teachings of the Ventari Tablet. Betrayed by Gavin, Vanilla first seeks guidance from Caithe, then pretends to join the Nightmare Court to spy on one of its meetings.

Afterward, Vanilla captures a recruiter of the Nightmare Court, promising to protect her if she says where Gavin took the stag. She does provide this information, but then Caithe kills the recruiter, to Vanilla's horror. Vanilla actually tried to stop Caithe, and even to kill her, but Caithe proved invulnerable. Following Caithe's commands only so far as to rescue the stag, Vanilla becomes alienated from the Cycle of Night, even as she represents its principles. From that moment forward she would not accept missions in the so-called personal story designed for Sylvari characters, but would explore the whole wide world, doing missions for local quest-givers, and collecting natural resources for Mr. Sims. She had decided that she suffered from a serious allergy—to deception—that could be managed only by staying away from allergenic plants like Caithe.

A crafting partnership

When Vanilla reached level 20 and I created the avatar based on William E. Sims, it took him 5 levels of experience to begin crafting. By the time Vanilla had reached 25, much of her effort was devoted to delivering many kinds of natural resource into their shared bank account, initially vegetables and meat for cooking, then cloth and leather for tailoring. She also provided most of the money Mr. Sims used to buy other supplies, such as salt and baking powder. An avatar in *Guild Wars 2* can practice just two crafting professions at any given time, and Mr. Sims began with cooking and tailoring, but tried them all in time. Tailoring was chosen as his second craft not only because it created the kind of clothing that could be worn by both necromancers and elementalists, but more importantly because Mr. Sims could quickly make several 8-slot jute bags to increase his own and Vanilla's capacity to carry raw materials scavenged from the environment.

The raw material for each bag is 10 bolts of jute, each of which is made from 2 scraps of jute, which are looted from the bodies of defeated enemies, in one of three different ways. First, a few low-level enemies occasionally provide a scrap of jute directly. Second, at other times, loot will be in the form of a sack, which when opened provides jute. Third, when a piece of clothing is looted, and the avatar would not benefit from wearing it, the clothing can either be sold or materials salvaged from it by use of a slightly costly salvage kit, sometimes extracting a scrap of jute. Aside from the bags, the products of tailoring did not seem very useful, because Mr. Sims did not need to wear increasingly protective clothing since he stayed in safe cities, and Vanilla could loot or buy higher level clothing than he could produce, so Mr. Sims abandoned tailoring and took up a profession he found much more interesting, becoming an artificer. Below are listed the eight crafting professions, with the words used by trainers to describe them. In parentheses are the number of recipes he collected (although he did not have the skill to use all of them outside cooking and artificer), and the skill-specific experience levels reached.

> Armorsmith: "War's everywhere, and demand for armor is high. It's time to train up a new generation of armorsmiths." (44, 50)
>
> Artificer: "Artificers are always in demand. It takes extreme concentration and patience to craft magical items." (228, 400)
>
> Cook: "Cooking has many recipes to master. Also, the ingredients come from all over the world and can be expensive." (152, 400)
>
> Huntsman: "I can train you to be a huntsman and make superior weapons like guns, bows, warhorns, and torches." (119, 50)
>
> Jeweler: "Harness the beauty of jewels and you unleash their potency to gain that edge in combat." (45, 100)
>
> Leatherworker: "A leatherworker knows how to make armor that protects you in comfort and style as your travel the world. Interested?" (44, 50)
>
> Tailor: "To be a tailor and make a truly fine garment, you need good materials and a strong stitch. Shall I teach you?" (39, 54)
>
> Weaponsmith: "Ah, the heat of the forge—where true weapons are born! Train with me and every blade, mace, or hammer you make will bring you glory." (143, 50)

My grandfather Sims in fact cultivated many hobbies, some thoroughly and some only superficially. In addition to horticulture, he had beehives, although remarkably they were stolen from him. In addition to reading extensively in history, he was a philatelist, and he believed that his collection contained all but four of the postage stamps of the Confederate States of America, harmonizing with his readings in Civil War history. He loved classical music, expressed not only by the violin sitting on the

DOI: 10.1057/9781137490599.0009

grand piano in the living room, but also by his extensive collection of recordings and the fact that like a few other fans of Jean Sibelius, he always sent that composer one fine cigar on his birthday. Especially relevant here, he was an expert chess player, active in local competitions, and had an extensive collection of chess journals. During his crafting work, I constantly sought online advice on what new recipes to learn, and what materials would be needed, comparable to him consulting the chess journals.

Cooking, his second profession, can illustrate the challenges, and he ultimately became both chef and artificer at level 400, the maximum skill level. He was not, in real life, an amateur cook, but did craft his own cigarettes from a collection of exotic tobaccos, and he collected many artifacts like an Egyptian scarab and a simulated Roman dinner bell that were like the creations of an artificer. The guidebook for *Guild Wars 2* warns that cooking is not easy, and indeed that crafting is a hobby more than a path to worldly success.[8]

The materials for cooking have the widest range of sources. Killing animals sometimes provides meat, many vegetables can be harvested from plants growing hither and yon, and on rare occasions chopping down a tree provides walnuts or cinnamon sticks. A few very common ingredients can be bought from master chef NPC vendors, such as packets of salt. Cooking requires being at a cooking fire and combining ingredients. For example, one packet of salt from a vendor combined with one potato harvested in the field produces potato fries. Cooking increases both general experience on its 1–80 scale, and experience in the specific craft on its 1–400 scale, but a given recipe stops contributing to both kinds of experience much above the level at which an avatar could begin crafting it. Higher level recipes require higher level ingredients, so Vanilla's experience needed to increase so that her husband's could as well.

For cooking, but none of the other crafts, some ingredients can be obtained only by purchase from NPCs out in the field, who would refuse to do business until the avatar had completed a particular mission for that NPC. There were two examples in the level 60–70 Fireheart Rise region near Apostate's Waypoint. Chief Wupwup, a level 63 NPC questgiver, asked Vanilla to enter a dangerous cave, battle bats, and harvest truffles to feed to his warthogs. Once she had done this, he would sell her various things, including bags of horseradish root costing 112 karma, a secondary currency earned doing missions and not convertible into

DOI: 10.1057/9781137490599.0009

the main currency used on the player auction house as well as in buying from many NPC vendors or paying for teleports. Some distance north-west stood a level 64 colleague of his, Chief Nrocroc, who would sell bags of peaches at a cost of 154 karma, but only after Vanilla had harvested for him many prickleberries that were not only dangerous to pick but also surrounded by roaming bears.

The peaches were especially useful to Mr. Sims. While some recipes are automatically provided to a cook, and others can be bought, many must be discovered by trying various combinations of ingredients inside the cooking system interface. While Mr. Sims liked to experiment based on his intuitions, he often looked up recipes online, and made sure that he had the necessary ingredients to "discover" them. Peach tarts required 1 peach, 1 bag of sugar, 1 stick of butter, and 1 ball of dough. Vanilla purchased the peaches from Chief Nrocroc and sent both them and money to her husband, who could buy sugar from a vendor at 8 coins per bag in lots of 10. Sticks of butter could be obtained from loot bags, but not often, so he would buy them from the auction house. As of August 10, 2013, tens of thousands of sticks of butter were available, 2,117 at the lowest price of 30 coins per stick. A ball of dough could be cooked up from a jug of water and bag of flour, which could be purchased from the vendor for 8 coins each, plus one stick of butter, so each ball of dough cost 46 coins. Discovery of peach tarts raised Mr. Sims's cooking expertise to level 364, and he kept making them until no peaches were left.

At cooking level 375 Mr. Sims fiddled around with combinations of various vegetables Vanilla had harvested from the countryside, discovering how to make a bowl of winter vegetable mix, from 1 rutabaga, 1 parsnip, 1 turnip, and 1 potato. Various other recipes kept him busy until he no longer had any ingredients that could advance his experience. At this point Vanilla returned from her wanderings to Chief Nrocroc and bought some more peaches, which allowed Mr. Sims to "discover" peach pie filling, which required 1 peach, 1 bag of flour, 1 bag of sugar, and 1 stick of butter. He frantically churned out pie filling, never actually completing any of the pies, until achieving the maximum Master Cook level of 400. To prove that he could have mastered any of the other crafts, he took each one to level 50, jeweler, which he found a little interesting to 100, and artificer to 400. In the end, he was satisfied, treasuring the opportunity to reminiscence about his long-deceased wife, Mildred, revived in the virtual person of Vanilla.

DOI: 10.1057/9781137490599.0009

Conclusion

This chapter is a step toward the social veneration of deceased persons in virtual worlds, the logical extension of the work reported here but not yet the subject of serious research. While cousins on both side of my family have contributed information and encouragement, we have not attempted to enter a gameworld together, playing the roles of multiple deceased ancestors simultaneously. Had my sister not died in 1965, I could well imagine us today entering *Guild Wars 2*, she playing Mildred and I playing Mr. Sims, virtually co-present even if living hundreds of miles apart, and actually going on adventures together. I do know of families that use online games as a way of socializing despite living far from each other, and this phenomenon could become very common if people used games for a greater variety of meaningful purposes. Perhaps readers of this book will see the opportunity to become pioneers themselves, using an appropriately selected gameworld both as a place to meet geographically distant relatives, and a means for communing with members of the family who have already departed this world.

Notes

1   Frederick Clifton Pierce, *Foster Genealogy* (Chicago: Press of W. B. Conkey, 1899), p. 604.
2   Hubert Rutherford Brown, *The Lawyers List* (New York: Brown, 1920), p. 225; Tamar Lewin, "Business and the Law: Smaller Firms Are Vanishing," *New York Times*, March 9, 1987.
3   Albert Kimsey Owen, *Integral Co-operation* (New York: Lovell, 1885); Ray Reynolds, *Cat'spaw Utopia* (San Bernardino, CA: Borgo, 1996).
4   William Sims Bainbridge, *eGods* (New York: Oxford University Press), pp. 189–193.
5   wiki.guildwars2.com/wiki/Sylvari.
6   Claude Lévi-Strauss, *The Raw and the Cooked* (New York: Harper & Row, 1969).
7   wiki.guildwars2.com/wiki/Ventari_Tablet.
8   Michael Lummis, Kathleen Pleet, Edwin Kern, and Kurt Ricketts, *Guild Wars 2* (Indianapolis: BradyGames, 2012), p. 284.

8
Enduring Horror (*Age of Conan*)

Abstract: *The three concluding chapters memorialize three members of the same family who died together in a horrible accident, each expressing a very different reaction to an identical death. This chapter concerns the wife; the next chapter concerns the husband, and the final chapter, their daughter. Every human being embodies culture, yet modern societies are culturally complex tapestries of interwoven cultural strands. This chapter illustrates how a computer game may be suitable for revival of a particular sattva precisely because it belongs to a subculture that was very important to her in real life. The game is the MMO* Age of Conan *and the sattva was a fan not of Robert Howard, the author of Conan whose own life ended in a psychotic suicide, but of A. Merritt, a much more successful author in the same fantasy-horror tradition, that also included H. P. Lovecraft. Appropriately, the particular religion that she joined in* Age of Conan *focused on resurrection not through the ministry of a merciful god, but in the application of horrible magic. As a Stygian necromancer, she constantly resurrected corpses to serve as her bodyguards, thus accomplishing transmigration, resurrection by means of technology, rather than religion.*

Bainbridge, William Sims. *An Information Technology Surrogate for Religion: The Veneration of Deceased Family in Online Games.* New York: Palgrave MacMillan, 2014.
DOI: 10.1057/9781137490599.0010.

> Transmigration: Resurrection by means of technology, thus magi-
> cal rather than religious.

Every human being embodies culture, yet modern societies are culturally complex tapestries of interwoven cultural strands. This chapter
illustrates how a computer game may be suitable for revival of a
particular sattva precisely because it belongs to a subculture that was
very important to that person in real life. The game is the MMO *Age of
Conan* (AoC), and the sattva was derived from my mother, Barbara Sims
Bainbridge (1914–1965), who was an avid reader of fantasy literature. She
was not in fact a fan of the Conan novels by Robert E. Howard, which I
believe she found too brutal, but of other authors belonging to the same
general tradition. The manner of her death was horrible, rendering the
horror in Howard's writing and in his suicide even more appropriate for
this revival. Thus the appropriate beginning is a true-life horror story,
redolent with symbolism. Most especially, the particular religion that
she joined in AoC focused on resurrection not through the ministry of a
merciful god, but in the application of horrible magic.

Dwellers in the Mirage

Barbara learned horticulture from her father, and when he died she
inherited from him a number of plants, including a beautiful Japanese
jade tree. Her most distinctive act of memorial for him was to replace a
small porch off the library of her home on Lucas Point, Old Greenwich,
Connecticut, with a greenhouse. She could read a book or watch television in the library, then walk but a few steps into the greenhouse to tend to
the plants, which included a Venus fly-trap and several orchids. In winter,
icicles would form on the gutter over the greenhouse, and crash down,
breaking the glass, so a rather crude heating wire was wrapped around
the gutter, to prevent the ice formation. Nobody remembered to unplug
it, and in the night of May 14, 1965, the wire short-circuited, causing the
unshielded power cable in the wall to flare and set the wood ablaze.

   She, her husband, and their daughter died, other members of the family
learning of the tragedy from television news the next day. The ripples
from these three drops of life that fell into the sea of death were feeble,
yet persist. The website of a local ladies' group lists its annual awards,
including: "A Revere pitcher, in memory of Mrs. William Bainbridge,

DOI: 10.1057/9781137490599.0010

may be awarded annually to a Garden Club member for outstanding work in Horticulture, exemplifying the purpose of the Garden Club of Old Greenwich."¹ Yet consider the irony! A greenhouse dedicated to life caused death. The only survivor was the jade tree.

An obscure detail can be the entry point for analysis. On the built-in bookshelves just to the right of the greenhouse, above a window, was Barbara's collection of the novels of her favorite author, A. Merritt, including autographed first editions. The paper was turned to ash, yet the novels can be read today online from Gutenberg.² One, titled *Dwellers in the Mirage*, could be especially relevant here, because it involves mystical spirit possession and multiple realities, quite comparable to avatars of sattvas in virtual worlds. But her favorite novel was *The Ship of Ishtar*, and I commemorated that fact by writing the Wikipedia article for that one of Merritt's works, signing her name to it:

> The archaeologist hero, Kenton, receives a mysterious ancient Babylonian artifact, which he discovers contains an incredibly detailed model of a ship. A dizzy spell casts Kenton onto the deck of the ship, which becomes a full-sized vessel sailing an eternal sea. At one end is Sharane the assistant priestess of Ishtar and her female minions, and at the other is Klaneth the assistant priest of Nergal and his male minions, representatives of two opposed deities. None of them can cross an invisible barrier at the midline of the ship, but Kenton can. His arrival destabilizes a situation that had been frozen for 6,000 years, and fantastic adventures ensue.
>
> The novel is not only a rousing fantasy adventure story, but a philosophi-cal exploration of the relationship between material reality and the abstract concepts through which humans struggle to understand it. The reason the ship has been frozen in time is that Zarpanit the head priestess of Ishtar and Alusar the head priest of Nergal fell in love, and were in the midst of making love when their deities possessed them. This placed the hostile deities in an untenable position, especially as they represented cosmic forces that must be kept separate. The result was an imbalance between stability and instability in the universe, freezing the ship in time and rendering unstable its connection to the reality inhabited by the reader.³

Merritt belonged to the same literary subculture as Howard, exemplified by H. P. Lovecraft, supernatural fantasy fiction with intense elements of horror. Indeed, the three authors once wrote a story together, in collabo-ration with C. L. Moore and Frank Belknap Long. Titled "The Challenge from Beyond," it was a round-robin story, in which Moore wrote the first section; then she passed it to Merritt to write the second, followed

DOI: 10.1057/9781137490599.0010

by Lovecraft, Howard, and Long in that order.[4] The title could be the name of their entire school of literature, because if taken seriously their literature describes a supernatural faith, albeit one that lacks hope and cathedrals. The cultural orientation of the Conan stories and indeed the entire genre is quasi-historical or anthropological, imagining that the most horrifying supernatural beliefs of real or imagined pre-Christian societies were somehow true.

Barbara also enjoyed historical novels, often set in ancient times, which did not promote alternative supernaturalisms, yet possessed surreal qualities. One of her favorites was *Andivius Hedulio* by Edward Lucas White. In a remarkable appendix, White claims that he dreamed this novel, scene by scene. Like Howard, White was a suicide, killing himself exactly seven years after the death of his beloved wife. Another of Barbara's favorites was *The Last Days of Pompeii* by Edward Bulwer-Lytton, because she loved one of the central characters, Blind Nydia. The novel introduces Nydia as a sightless flower-girl singing a sweet song, but later she is able to save many normal residents of Pompeii when the volcano erupts, because she can find her way to safety without seeing, and their sight is obscured by the ashes.

Barbara possessed a black and white photogravure print showing Blind Nydia from that novel, which she framed and hung on our wall. A beautiful woman, her eyes closed and head tipped back, walks across a mosaic floor, carrying a plate of flowers, unaware that one blossom has dropped. The print is gone, but from memory I was able to use Internet to identify the original precisely. In 2009 Southeby's had sold the original oil painting by Baron Cuno von Bodenhausen for $11,875 under the more abstract name, "Maiden in a Classical Interior." Gutenberg not only offers the novel, but allows us to count how often Nydia is named in it, fully 279 times, a sign of how profoundly her story might impress a young girl reading about how a disability became an ability.[5]

Another of Barbara's favorite novels was *The Cat of Bubastes* by G. A. Henty. As a teenager, she had composed a short poem, beginning something like, "G. A. Henty wrote books twenty for little girls like me." While much milder in tone than the Conan novels, it has some parallels, concerning the story of an Eastern European prince, brought as a slave to Egypt around 1450 BC during the reign of pharaoh Thutmose III. His father, the king, was slain in battle attempting to halt the Egyptian invasion, and then his mother, the queen, committed suicide to avoid being captured, but not before writing a farewell missive to him:

DOI: 10.1057/9781137490599.0010

You will doubtless, my son, be carried away captive into Egypt, but you may yet escape some day and rejoin your people, or may meet with some lot in which you may find contentment or even happiness there. At any rate, my last words to you are, bear patiently whatever may befall you, remember always that your father was king of the Rebu, and whatever your station in life may be, try to be worthy of the rank to which you were born. There is no greater happiness on a throne than in a cottage. Men make their own happiness, and a man may be respected even though only a slave. May the gods of your country preside over and protect you always.[6]

Most MMOs involve a lot of killing, but few make death and despair so prominent in the stories as does AoC, so it was an ideal venue for revival of Barbara, using the nickname she preferred, *Simsey*. This was how she signed her page in the high school graduating class yearbook: "We live and learn, so they say. I've lived but not learned—and you?"

A Stygian necromancer

Earlier, I had explored AoC through four characters, the most prominent of which was based on a priest of the god Mitra named Orastes in Robert E. Howard's Conan novel, *The Hour of the Dragon*, which an early publisher had renamed *Conan the Conqueror*.[7] I briefly tried a necromancer who followed the competing snake god of Stygia. That gave me the basis for deciding Simsey needed to be a Stygian necromancer. As one, she could explore the decidedly non-Christian immortality technology of *spirit summoning*, the antonym of exorcism that is not uncommon in other religious cultures around the world.[8] The AoC Wiki describes the class thus:

> Necromancers summon and command the undead and they are legion. Their ghoulish minions are capable of tearing men apart or casting their own death magic. The rotten corpses of the dead follow, wherever the necromancer leads. Evil and twisted Necromancers bring the cursed and dead back from beyond the mortal realm to do their bidding. The dark magic wielded by necromancers ranges from the unholy to pestilent corruption and the freezing touch of death. Through careful study they can develop the ability to call corpses from the earth to rise up and surround a foe or even attain lichdom, turning themselves into terrifying undead archmages.[9]

The standard character backstory, which fit Orastes very well, was that the player's avatar undergoes a near-death experience, washes up on

DOI: 10.1057/9781137490599.0010

a beach near the town of Tortage in the Barachan Isles, which may possibly be a fantasy version of Tortuga in the Caribbean, and Barbara had visited the Caribbean at least twice. On one of those visits she was—in real life—held prisoner. She and my father were in Havana, Cuba, in the last days of the Batista regime. As innocent American tourists, one evening they went nightclub-hopping, and by mistake entered one that was closed, where a meeting of Castro's revolutionaries was in progress. They were held only a short while, but it was a dramatic experience.

Real life seldom emulates fiction stories, but sometimes it really does. Barbara attended Spence then Brearley, two private day schools for girls that have maintained their high reputations until the present day. A story she delighted to tell about her years at Brearley concerned an essay she wrote about her summer experiences that the teacher flunked, because it concerned her kidnapping and thus clearly could not be true. However, she actually had been kidnapped that summer. An employee of the Sims family, Eddie Foo from China, had become enamored of her and in a confused state of mind had held the family at gunpoint for several hours, until her father was able to convince Eddie to let him go for some liquor, but he returned with the police instead. Eddie was taken to Ellis Island, and deported.

There is something captivating, in the negative sense of the term, about games like AoC that require completion of specific missions to progress in the normal way. When Simsey washed up on that Tortage beach, she wanted to escape as soon as she could. In the standard game-play the avatar must go through 20 levels of missions in Tortage, and follow a main story line from there onward, regaining lost memories. I wanted Simsey to explore all the experience levels from 1 to the level cap of 80, but was not interested in redoing all of the main story line, and preferred to assume that her memory was intact. Guided by online forums, she took a secret alternative exit from Tortage at level 17.

As a necromancer, when she gained levels, she gained the ability to summon different kinds of undead minions, which she would order to attack enemies as she hurled killing spells, and when necessary drank potions to restore her health in combat and the magical mana that was consumed by her spells. Many of her minions were rotting corpses, while the others were monstrous magicians. Here is the full list she had acquired by experience level 80 and 170 hours, adapting the descriptions

DOI: 10.1057/9781137490599.0010

from those in the game interface, with the level at which she gained each in parentheses:

Undead Minions:

Mutilator (5): Inflicts bleeding wounds, that may combine into slashing attacks.

Corruptor (20): Basic close-range attack with a chance of causing unholy damage.

Blighted One (25): Close-range attacks inflict mana damage.

Necrotic Bomb (35): Close-range attacks with some chance of exploding, and can be made to explode by the Necrotic Detonation spell.

Harvester (45): Increases the mana and stamina of the necromancer's team, described as a "blasphemy."

Life-Stealer (50): Transfers life from the enemy to the necromancer's team.

Deathless Acolytes:

Magus (30): Does a small amount of splash damage around its primary target.

Arcanist (45): Augmenting the damage done by the necromancer's team.

Reaper (60): Their spells have a chance of draining life from the target and healing the necromancer and their associates.

Dread Archmages:

Archmagus (65): Strikes enemies over a large area.

Blood Arcanist (80): Can heal allies by sacrificing its own life.

Necromancers can have more than one active minion at a given moment. Simsey had eight points she could use to summon minions, and some necromancers earned a couple more in difficult missions. Each Undead Minion required one point, so at level 50 she could have one each of all six of them, plus two duplications, combining their various advantages, or she could have had eight of just one type. Deathless Acolytes required two points each, and from level 45 to 60 Simsey tended to have two Maguses and two Arcanists, simply because she found more than four minions to be a confusing crowd. Later she used two Arcanists and two Reapers. Undead Minions run up and attack the enemy at close range, and are described as "mindless," while Deathless Acolytes are undead sorcerers who stand at a distance and like Simsey herself cast damaging spells. Notice that resurrected sorcerers possessed at least a portion of their original minds, and the goal of every Stygian sorcerer was to gain sufficient magical power to summon themselves back to life after death.

DOI: 10.1057/9781137490599.0010

When selecting the necromancer class in the creation of Simsey, I also had to select her race. When I first explored AoC, there were three starting races. The Aquilonians seemed most civilized, a fantasy hybrid of ancient Greco-Roman culture and perhaps Carolingian Franks, centered in a large city named Tarantia and conceptualizing their god Mitra as benign if a bit distant. The Cimmerians, who were modelled on Celtic or Norse barbarians and to whom Conan belonged, had an even more distant and brutal god, Crom. The Stygians, who had elements of ancient Egyptian and Babylonian culture, were obsessed with the occult and adored the destructive snake god, Set. When Simsey entered AoC, a fourth race had been added to which avatars could belong, the Khitan, based on culture from China and Korea and perhaps intended to attract players from those nations.

A necromancer could belong to either the Stygian or Khitan races, but Barbara was fascinated by ancient Egypt, so naturally she was Stygian. The snake god, Set, has the name of one of the ancient Egyptian deities, who, however, was not a serpent. The small but impressive city of the Stygians in AoC is named Khemi, reminiscent of Khemit, the name of ancient Egypt, meaning *the black land.*

Realms of lust and horror

There are two explanations for why Robert E. Howard filled the Conan stories with ancient horror: commercial and psychological. Writing in the early years of the Great Depression, he had great difficulty earning a living. He apparently liked writing less fanciful stories about adventure and sports, but the Conan stories sold, and he was forced to follow the advice of the editors who bought them. This was an extremely stressful livelihood; Howard's personal life was rather unsuccessful, and in retrospect that he might be diagnosed mentally ill. When he was a child, he and his mother agreed to die together, and as an adult when he learned his mother was dying, he shot himself.[10] Barbara's favorite author, A. Merritt, could hardly be more different. Among the most successful journalists of his period, he was quite prosperous, emotionally stable, and possessing the time and mental equilibrium to design his novels carefully. Almost all of the Conan stories are rather short, each focused on one or another psychotic episode, and consisting of lurid language and emotional outpouring of fear, rage, and lust.

DOI: 10.1057/9781137490599.0010

Howard's suicide came immediately after the publication of *Conan the Conqueror*, an ironic title given that Howard himself had been conquered by life. But, remarkably, Conan lived on. In the fiction stories and AoC, Conan became king of Aquilonia, but in reality he became the governor of California. Of course I refer to the movie actor Arnold Schwarzenegger who played the title role in *Conan the Barbarian* and *Conan the Destroyer* in the 1980s, before morphing into a politician. In a sense, then, Schwarzenegger was an avatar of Conan.

More to the point here, after Howard's death, other authors began writing Conan stories. Much of the credit goes to L. Sprague de Camp, a rather fine fiction writer and historian, who edited and expanded some of Howard's manuscripts before writing his own Conan stories. When an avatar in AoC goes from one zone or instance to another, a flash screen displays the name of the destination plus some descriptive text. Three examples cite Howard's stories, *The Hour of the Dragon*, "The Scarlet Citadel," and "The Tower of the Elephant." Another quotes from his essay about Conan's fictional world, "The Hyborian Age." Others cite three Conan stories by L. Sprague de Camp and Lin Carter, "The Witch of the Mists," "Conan of Aquilonia," and "Conan of the Isles." Another cites the novel *Conan the Valorous* by John Maddox Roberts. Fiction by many other authors, plus a slew of Conan comic books and games, complete a rather vast Conanic mythos.

When AoC first launched it was rated "M" for mature, and a question for the game designers was how closely they should emulate the rather psychotic violence and eroticism in the original stories by Robert E. Howard. When I first played, drops of blood would splash across the screen during battles, but this feature had been removed by the time Simsey entered years later. Rape and sexualized torture are common in his stories, and the main quest arc in Tortage involved a donation of blood from a prostitute substituted for the blood of a virgin in a human sacrifice, in order to cause ruin to the enemies performing that ritual. Simsey's Undead Minions are rotting corpses, and a few of the quest-givers in AoC have lost a limb to combat, or indeed, are themselves dead. One is a severed head on a pole.

Missions in the Thunder River region of Aquilonia, designed for avatars in the level 60–70 range, illustrate the gruesome extremes that can be found throughout AoC. A quest-giver named Captain Tiberius first sent Simsey to kill 14 enemy scouts, then assassinate Voteporix, the leader of one of their factions, and plant a false clew that another faction

DOI: 10.1057/9781137490599.0010

was responsible. His next assignment, "A Gruesome Death," was to assassinate one of the secondary enemy leaders, Evodius. However, this proved impossible, because a pack of wild dogs had already dismembered Evodius, so the mission became killing enough dogs to reach the corpse and see how horrible it looked. In "Forbidden Longing," quest-giver Hodong asked Simsey to rescue his beloved, Nak Rang, from a mercenary camp. But all Simsey found was the girl's severed head on a platter. In "The Girl with no Fear," Simsey was sent to rescue Ulla, but found her crucified on a tree, horribly wounded. Her dying words assigned Simsey the task of killing ten of her torturers: "Aye, the misty domain of Crom ... awaits, but I'd not go to the darkness without ... vengeance. Find those cowards who'd use a blade against a woman restrained and ... bleed them. Splash their blood on the walls of their ... fortress. Let them see what the life of a single ... Cimmerian costs. Then I can ... go to Crom's realm with a smile. Bleed them well, friend..."

Every virtual world can be considered from the viewpoint of a geographer, and Simsey invested much time exploring two Stygian zones of the type called adventure regions, that offer many quests, Khopshef Province and Kheshatta. On the eastern side of Khopshef stands Pyramid of the Ancients, not a pharaoh's tomb but an instance of the type called a dungeon that contains many quests leading to a duel with a boss. Strikingly, the main lower level is inhabited by obese eunuchs guarding imprisoned harem girls, and such lovelies as a quest-giver who eats only human eyeballs. Higher floors contain torture chambers and hallways polluted with poison gas. Kheshatta is a pseudo-Egyptian city surrounded by wasteland, the headquarters of black magicians. Among the more demanding mission arcs was a duel with a Khitan sorcerer named Gildong. "Khitan" of course means "Chinese," and Simsey thought of him as a resurrection of Eddie Foo, thus deserving to be shamed by her Stygian powers. He had created seven "reflections" of himself, *avatars* to use the Hindu word, and she would need to destroy each of them before facing Gildong himself in a duel to the death, which, however, he chickened out of!

Harvesting and crafting

When Simsey escaped Tortage, she entered the wider world at Khemi, the religious capital of Stygia where priests of Set the Serpent God preside.

DOI: 10.1057/9781137490599.0010

The Howard story "Queen of the Black Coast" mentions entering "the broad bay where the Styx river emptied its gigantic flood into the ocean, and the massive black castles of Khemi loomed over the blue waters."[11] The novel *The Hour of the Dragon* uses the name Khemi 14 times, notably referring to "the sea-washed castles of black-walled Khemi" and offering a one-paragraph geography lesson:

> The river was the Styx, the real border of Stygia. Khemi was Stygia's greatest port, and at that time her most important city. The king dwelt at more ancient Luxur, but in Khemi reigned the priestcraft; though men said the center of their dark religion lay far inland, in a mysterious, deserted city near the bank of the Styx. This river, springing from some nameless source far in the unknown lands south of Stygia, ran northward for a thousand miles before it turned and flowed westward for some hundreds of miles, to empty at last into the ocean.[12]

In Greek legend, the Styx was the boundary between this life and the afterlife of Hades, but for Howard it also represented the Nile. In AoC, Khemi is not dark in color, but sandy, a stucco island town that possesses a full set of services for players and connections to Tarantia in Aquilonia and to the other zones of Stygia. While a few missions took place in Khemi, mainly it was a transportation hub and commercial center, including access to a player-to-player market that Simsey used extensively. She set Khemi as her home base, which meant that she could teleport there from anywhere, whether to do business or to travel to a zone that was not directly connected to the one she was in. Very often, she would commute between Khemi and Purple Lotus Swamp, a nonadventure zone serving as the harvesting region for Stygia and containing Nakaset Village, essentially a school town with trainers for all harvesting and crafting professions. In "The Scarlet Citadel," Howard referred to the paralyzing "juice of the purple lotus which grows in the ghost-haunted swamps of southern Stygia."[13]

Given her goal to reach the level 80 experience cap and explore much of the world of Conan, Simsey resolved to master all six harvesting professions. At levels 20, 50, and 70, she would carry out missions for trainers to gain the ability to collect special resources from the environment whenever she wanted, and occasionally by chance rare resources as well. This list gives the three main resources for each, in order from first to third:

DOI: 10.1057/9781137490599.0010

Mining: copper, iron, duskmetal
Prospecting: silver, electrum, gold
Stonecutting: sandstone, granite, basalt
Woodcutting: ash, yew, oak
Weaving: cotton, silk, ironsilk
Skinning: rough leather, calloused leather, gnarled leather

The first three require hammering on rock nodes, widely distributed across adventure zones as well as the swamp, while woodcutting naturally requires chopping on trees. Harvesting cotton requires hand picking from bushes. All these resources are located on the map in the AoC interface, and working one might at random trigger an attack by an enemy. The varieties of silk and leather were harvested from dead enemies. Manufacturing crafts, which can be learned at level 40, use these and other resources collected from the environment or looted from dead enemies.

Only two of the five crafts can be practiced, but Simsey made two switches so she gained at least some experience with four, leaving out weaponsmithing. In early adulthood, Barbara had enjoyed dressmaking, which also was an economic way of making decent if not stylish clothing in the 1940s. The nearest thing in AoC was armorsmithing, and she developed her skills until she was able to make silk robes for herself to wear. She briefly tried gemcutting, but switched to alchemy because it was both useful and closest to her life-long craft and hobby, cooking. Later, when she joined a guild named the Red Pirates that had its own rather huge city, she dropped armorsmithing for architecture, hoping to help add additional buildings. As it turned out, both armorsmithing and architecture were very costly to learn, the first because it required great quantities of leather to complete all the projects assigned by the teacher, and architecture because each structure required a costly plan diagram, and one needed very many of them to qualify for graduation at each instruction grade.

Alchemy was the one craft Simsey was able to take near the highest skill level, and indeed she had been an avoid gourmet cook in real life, with files of recipes clipped from magazines or written on file cards in consultation with friends. She herself used two kinds of alchemy product, liquors that for a significant period of time increased her maximum health and mana plus their out-of-combat restoration rate, and potions that would restore health or mana as needed during combat. Some of the ingredients were looted from corpses of enemies, or bought in the market at low prices from other players who had looted them, and others were very cheap to buy from specialized NPC vendors. Simsey imagined that she could make lots of money selling potions in the market, but unfortunately it turned out that too few buyers and too many sellers caused the prices to be unprofitably low.

Conclusion

Upon reaching the maximum level 80 of experience, Simsey decided that it was time to close the book on Conan. She checked out the features of her final minion, the Blood Arcanist, and discovered that she could not complete her last alchemy training session because her guild lacked a level III alchemy laboratory. She had lived and learned, but never found the consolation in the face of death claimed by popular religion. No, if death is horrible, and no happy afterlife really exists for mortals, then Heaven is an insulting illusion. We must feel fear, but not let it conquer us. Honestly, I am not sure what truths she would say she had learned from life, were she able to speak to us again. But I suspect that she would have praised all forms of fiction that ennoble human existence through their artistic qualities, but never pretend they are anything more than fiction.

Notes

1   gardenclubofoldgreenwich.org/2010awardwinners.html.
2   gutenberg.net.au/ebooks01/0100151.txt.
3   en.wikipedia.org/wiki/The_Ship_of_Ishtar.
4   C. L. Moore, Abraham Merritt, H. P. Lovecraft, Robert E. Howard, and Frank Belknap Long, "The Challenge from Beyond." *Fantasy Magazine*, September 1935, 5(4): 221–229.
5   www.gutenberg.org/cache/epub/1565/pg1565.txt
6   G. A. Henty, *The Cat of Bubastes* (London: Blackie, 1889), p. 48.
7   William Sims Bainbridge, *eGods: Faith Versus Fantasy in Computer Gaming* (New York: Oxford University Press, 2013), pp. 111–115.
8   Kirsten W. Endres, "Engaging the Spirits of the Dead." *The Journal of the Royal Anthropological Institute*, 2008, 14(4): 755–773.
9   aoc.wikia.com/wiki/Necromancers
10   L. Sprague De Camp, Catherine Crook de Camp, and Jane Whittington Griffin, *Dark Valley Destiny: The Life of Robert E. Howard* (New York: Bluejay, 1983).

DOI: 10.1057/9781137490599.0010

11   Robert E. Howard, *The Coming of Conan the Cimmerian* (New York: Random House, 2002), p. 124.

12   Robert E. Howard, *The Bloody Crown of Conan* (New York: Random House, 2003), pp. 189, 203.

13   Howard, *The Coming of Conan the Cimmerian*, p. 88.

DOI: 10.1057/9781137490599.0010

9

Insuring Hope (*Elder Scrolls Online*)

Abstract: *The husband of the woman featured in the previous chapter was an executive of a major life insurance corporation, and thus his main theme as an avatar was protecting and rescuing. A fundamental principle of this book is quite similar, preservation, preventing a person from being totally destroyed at death, by allowing the deceased to continue to contribute to the living. Evidence of his actual death scene suggests that he valiantly attempted to save his daughter, but failed, so the goal of role-playing here will be to locate and protect an avatar based on his wife. The life insurance company that employed him was at the time a mutual corporation, existing entirely for the policyholders and having no stockholders, thus existing at some variance with modern capitalism and representing a community more than financial interests. The MMO is the very new* Elder Scrolls Online, *and his avatar actually entered it before its official launch, serving as a beta tester and thus expressing a sense of urgency with saving his wife, against all odds.*

Bainbridge, William Sims. *An Information Technology Surrogate for Religion: The Veneration of Deceased Family in Online Games.* New York: Palgrave MacMillan, 2014.
DOI: 10.1057/9781137490599.0011

> Preservation: Preventing a person from being totally destroyed at death, by allowing the deceased to continue to contribute to the living.

William Wheeler Bainbridge (1914–1965) was actually well prepared to become a character in *Elder Scrolls Online*, because in many respects he represented ancient feudal traditions, never attending a plebian public school and possessing many skills that would have suited a knight centuries ago. He first attended the Friends' Seminary in New York City, a Quaker academy that today says it cultivates the Inner Light, believing that God exists within every person: "Guided by the ideals of integrity, peace, equality and simplicity, and by our commitment to diversity, we do more than prepare students for the world that is: we help them bring about the world that ought to be."[1] At the time of his death he was an executive of a life insurance corporation, a field he privately admitted should really be called death insurance. His work provided practical hope that the harm caused by death could be minimized, while religion offers far less reliable hope that it can be completely overcome, but not in a way that can be verified. This chapter explores the tension between these two ideologies, calling the real-world sattva *WWB*, and the virtual-world avatar *William*.

A member of the equestrian class

WWB entered Mohegan Lake Military School at Mohegan Lake, New York, in 1925 and graduated in 1932, serving his last two years as Senior Cadet Officer. He was, in a very real sense, the "last of the Mohegans," because this school closed down just when he graduated. He had been sent there because it was the boarding school his father had attended many decades earlier, and near its demise had become more of a marching academy, than an academic institution, thus providing him a rather poor education. Yet as an adult, William loved to read historical novels.

At school, he excelled in sports of all kinds, especially football, basketball, and baseball. In 1933 he entered Lafayette College, and transferred to New York University, where in 1937 he received both the degree of Bachelor of Science and the Business Certificate. This was the time of the Great Depression, but he was able to get a job as an underling at the Detroit office of The Equitable Life Assurance Society of the United

DOI: 10.1057/9781137490599.0011

States. Soon, he was able to prove himself to The Equitable, and get a better assignment working directly for the home office in New York City, responsible for selling group insurance in nearby Connecticut.

He entered the Army on March 30, 1944, as a private in the cavalry, having long been an expert horseman. He served in the First Cavalry at Fort Riley, Kansas, becoming corporal in November, 1944, and staff sergeant in March, 1945. He trained men and horses for service in the Pacific theater of the war, but never fought there himself. In later years he would look back on his military service with some ambivalence, telling anecdotes about failures, such as when a military dentist broke his jaw, which required him to communicate with his men for a few days only by blowing a whistle.

He often commented on the futility of war, noting that Fort Riley trained 20,000 men and horses on the assumption that they would been needed to battle the Japanese through the jungles of New Guinea, but once sent there all the horses promptly died of tropical diseases, and anyway the United States followed the better strategy of only taking a few of the port towns and letting many Japanese rot in the hinterland. He also would comment that the reason he tolerated the temporary lack of freedom as a military draftee was so that we would not live in a society where freedom was lacking all the time. Upon discharge from the cavalry, he returned to the Equitable, where he became Manager of the Group Casualty Coverages. Sociologist Viviana Zelizer has documented how life insurance arose in nineteenth-century America as a secular surrogate for religion's traditional function to deal with death, and the many missions in *Elder Scrolls Online* that involve rescuing people have a similar symbolism.[2]

A parent's job not only supports a child economically but also provides much of the cultural context in which that child develops. A tiny anecdote illustrates that point. One of my favorite dramatic radio programs when we lived in Bethel was *The FBI in Peace and War*, which was sponsored by The Equitable. Each week an advertisement would tell the listener to "go see your Equitable agent." Immediately, I would run downstairs, look at my father, and then run back up to hear the rest of the program.

By sponsoring *The FBI in Peace and War* for its entire existence, The Equitable implied that, like the real FBI, it protected the American public, just as my father protected me. Indeed, for once an advertising gimmick may have been true. At the time my father was employed by it, The

DOI: 10.1057/9781137490599.0011

Equitable was a *mutual* insurance company, which meant that it was owned by the policyholders and had no stockholders. That is to say, it existed at some distance from capitalism, even as it was embedded in the capitalist system.[3] While my father earned a good salary, it was not spectacular, and despite being a top executive he received no stock in a company that, after all, had none. Mutual insurance companies still exist today, although The Equitable no longer belongs to that idealistic category.

Transition

Elder Scrolls Online provided a perfect context for vicariously experiencing the fundamental meaning of my father's life and death. From the position of the three bodies in the ashes at Lucas Point, and the condition of the house, we can infer but not know with certainty the death experiences of the three people. It seems that all three had moved a short distance from their sleeping locations. Yet escape was difficult. Many of the upstairs windows were blocked by air conditioners. The main damage of the fire was downstairs, so it was difficult to descend by either stairway. Because of her heavy epilepsy medication, WWB's daughter may not have awakened, yet was found in a bathroom. Perhaps her father took her from her bed, but could not carry her downstairs, shutting her for protection in the bathroom just the other side of the stairs, then plunged downward seeking help. His body was found on the landing, only half way down.

I imagine he has been vainly trying to save his family ever since. Perhaps recently he sensed that his daughter would be revived by her brother in the last chapter of this book, so his own goal became protection of Simsey. The first challenge was to find her. He knew that she had been briefly revived inside the solo-player game, *Elder Scrolls IV: Oblivion*, and a related MMO was in preparation, *Elder Scrolls Online*.[4] So at the beginning of September 2013 he resolved to enter that virtual world, on the assumption that she would have traveled there within the *Elder Scrolls* universe. But ESO had not been released yet, so he volunteered to become a beta tester, while this MMO was still under development.

On September 6, 2013, William found himself locked in a dungeon cell in caverns, his body revived but his soul still lost, in a mysterious plane of existence called Oblivion. A quest arc named "Soul Shriven in Coldharbour" had him search the cell, then a mysterious transparent figure appeared, calling himself The Prophet and saying, "I am the past and the future, both. I am despair, and hope." William's next mission was to escape the cell, gain a weapon, and free the prophet from the Wailing Prison.

Immediately he encountered a woman named Lyris Titanborn, not transparent but possessing a solid body like his own. She told him that they both were dead, although reanimated, and must liberate the Prophet in order to save themselves and indeed the entire world. A friendly madman playing a lute advised them how to reach the Prophet's cell. Then Lyris informed William that the only way to release him was to take his place. A sudden realization struck William like a thunderbolt. Perhaps Lyris was really Simsey! Players usually take new identities inside role-playing games, and both he and Lyris were desperately seeking to escape death, just as he and Simsey had at Lucas Point. But she would not let him take the place of the Prophet, entering the cell herself and giving William the responsibility of escorting the Prophet to safety. He resolved to return and rescue Lyris as soon as he could learn the magical means for accomplishing this sacred goal.

After a dizzying transition, William found himself inside a large building, rushing forward with many other escaped prisoners, and hearing an uncertain message from the Prophet who had been sent to some other, distant destination. Stepping out on a balcony, he saw a village of the hardy Nord tribe, only then realizing that he himself belonged to it, and remembering that this must be Bleakrock Isle. Stumbling out of the village, he encountered a wounded hunter named Darj, who assigned a mission to him at a dragon shrine. But then reality waivered, and he was paralyzed for a few minutes. When he could move again, he killed a few wild beasts. A strange woman named Molla spoke words to him he did not fully understand, and he again was paralyzed. His grasp on life weakened, and he fell back into Oblivion.

On November 22, 2013, William was again reborn in that same cell, where the Prophet repeated the same words. He again met Lyris, and felt even more certain she was really Simsey. Again, she was locked in the cell that had held the Prophet, and again William's assignment was to help the Prophet escape. He understood his surroundings better this time, and saw that their exit was through a Rift to Tamriel.

In the village he encountered a woman named Rana, who was the local military commander, and he sensed in her some of Simsey's strength. An invasion seemed immanent, and Rana asked him to warn villagers across the island to evacuate. Later, beside a river, he again met Molla,

DOI: 10.1057/9781137490599.0011

who seemed to have had some of Simsey's imagination, because she asked him to use a magic wand on three squirrels, seeking them here and there in the wilderness. Remarkably, they turned out to be people who had been transformed by evil spells, and he saved them. He found 15 missing but untransformed villagers, entered caverns and cultic gardens, completed missions for many quest-givers he encountered, then found a portal to Oblivion deep within a mine. This gave him hope that he could use such a gateway to rescue Lyris, but now was not the time for that mission. Instead, he joined Rana to help villagers escape the island through a maze of tunnels. By ship they reached the mainland, then this reincarnation, too, ended.

On January 11, 2014, which happened to be the 100th birthday of WWB, his avatar again found himself in that same damn prison cell, half dead and totally discouraged. This time, he allowed despair to drown his hopes, and he refused to talk with the Prophet for this third time.

On April 23, 2014, William once again found himself in that cell, seeking within himself the strength to try again. He meditated, and remembered that Simsey's birthday was April 12, so now she was more than a century old as well. Again he spoke to the Prophet, met Lyris, and again was unable to liberate her. This time the portal did not take him directly to Bleakrock Isle, but to a city named Davon's Watch. But there he learned that he had been rescued by people from Bleakrock, who had found him in the sea, so he felt the obligation to go there immediately by ship, to thank them and provide whatever help they needed.

Back on Bleakrock Isle for the third time, he found fewer missions than the previous visit, but completed all the ones he received. His mind was much more clear than before, as if his soul were slowing returning to consciousness, but this caused him to be thoroughly horrified by the missions he performed immediately before helping Rana lead the villagers through the tunnels of escape, because in several the danger was fire. He thought back to the many winter evenings, throughout his life, when the family had enjoyed the light and warmth from a fireplace, often burning wood he himself had chopped. Yet now, fire seemed like complete destruction, total evil, lacking any virtue.

As before, he helped Rana lead the villagers through the escape tunnels to the ship that carried them to the mainland. There, she gave him the mission to run to a watchtower and tell soldiers to light signal fires, warning Devon's Watch that war is coming. He remembered the flames on Lucas Point, which had delivered death rather than merely warning of its approach. He paused briefly, gathering his energies, and wondering how he could complete his own sacred mission, to rescue Simsey, as war engulfed the world.

Life assurance

These events, taking place across many months, were the experience of participating in three beta tests of ESO, plus entering after its public launch. They set the terms of his resurrection, not merely that he sought the woman who had been his wife, but also that his goal in life was providing security. Three examples of specific adventures will set the stage for consideration of the main quest arc that begins with the rescue of Lyris Titanborn, missions that possess symbolic depth while requiring William to make decisions.

For example, visiting Cragwallow in the Eastmarch zone, William spoke with the local leader, Berj Stonehart, about a party the community was planning, starting the mission "Merriment and Mystery." His first task was simple enough, to talk to two cooks who were arguing about what to serve for the grand dinner, and help one of them. Kalogar Cookpot was a bearded man wearing a chef's cap, who advocated bear steak, "charred on the outside, bloody in the middle." William had had enough of charring and blood, so he next spoke with the female cook, Heggvir Sun-Hair, who advocated savory goat stew. Sensing in her some of Simsey's flair for cooking, William agreed. She asked him to bring back a living goat, from the nearby wilderness, enticing it with a herb rather than killing it. He located some goats, carefully killed some wolves to clear the way, then led one goat back to Heggvir. The decision between bear steak or goat stew determined how exactly William should help, but did not have great consequences. Heggvir then asked William to get some more mead, the local alcoholic drink, from the storeroom, getting the key from Ralduf Wolf-Kin. Unfortunately, Ralduf ashamedly admitted that a wild wolf had swallowed the key, so William would need to track and kill it. Next came a few minor assignments helping to get the party organized.

Then Berj Stonehart asked William to find Valding the Bard and tell him to start singing. In a cutscene, I could hear Valding say he was about to sing, but then William fell unconscious. When he awoke, he discovered that all participants in the party had blacked out, many of them were now dead, and Valding was missing. Searching for clues, he encountered a dying man, Lothgar Steady-Hand, whose sword and shield had been stolen. Thus began a good example of an ancillary mission, finding the lost items so Lothgar would enter the afterlife as a properly equipped warrior. They, the bard, and the solution to the mystery were in a series of caves, where the enemies were too strong, but William was lucky enough to be doing the mission beside two powerful strangers, so between them they slaughtered all their foes. It turned out that Valding the Bard was not in fact a bard, but a simple thief, who had found a magical lute he could play despite lacking skill. He did not realize that it would attract humanoid Riekling creatures, who locked him in a cell. William had the option to leave him there, or to let him out but kill him, or to release him under the promise he would surrender to Cragwallow justice. Given his value system William chose the last of these options.

Another time, in the missions "Trade Negotiations" and "The Trial of the Ghost Snake," William met a young woman named Tevynni Hedran, assistant to a merchant named Raston Vendil, who had gone to trade with the Mabrigash tribe, and had failed to return. Thinking this was a simple rescue mission, William agreed to talk with the tribe leader, with the expectation that this would lead to a duel. But conversations with the leader and a wise Mabrigash woman were peaceful, suggesting that the merchant had brashly violated some tribal customs. Then William spoke with Farseer Bodani, a woman he came to feel was the real tribal authority, who said: "This fool has pestered our hunters, importuned our wisewomen, and insulted me by demanding to speak to the man in charge of our tribe. I brook no challenges to my authority or disruptions to the Vale." While Bodani lacked Simsey's gentleness, he sensed some of the same power, through which some women allow their men to believe that authority rests with males who hunt in the wider world, when really it belongs to females who are both wise and far-seeing.

A conversation with Raston Vendil, whose arms were tied behind his back, proved the man's sins to be venial, and thus not deserving sacrifice of his life to the snake god. So, William accepted a mission from Farseer Bodani to collect eight bog rats, offer them at a shrine to the Ghost Snake, and complete whatever trial this god demanded. To William's surprise, the Ghost Snake was a huge spiritual being who spoke peacefully about good and evil, about being both constant and ever-changing, and about appearing to different peoples in different forms. After easily defeating a

DOI: 10.1057/9781137490599.0011

minion as a simple trial of his dedication, William returned to the tribe to tell Farseer Bodani that she was free to decide what should be done with the annoying merchant.

She, in turn, gave William the choice, symbolized by a Snake Totem. If he placed it in the campfire, the tribe would reject all merchants and remain isolated for the surrounding world. If he gave it to merchant Raston Vendil, the tribe would accept him as their one and only agent in trading with outsiders. Instead he chose a third option that had not initially been offered to him, returning the totem to Farseer Bodani with the understanding that merchant Raston Vendil would be freed, but his female assistant, Tevynni Hedran would herself become the agent trading for the tribe with the outside world.

In the mission pair "The Thin Ones" and "The Bargain's End," William entered Stillrise Village, which endures some strange necromancer curse, speaking with a beautiful woman named Chieftain Suhlak. She tasked him to enter the cellars of three huts, to kill Worm Cult lieutenants. When he returned to tell her the job was done, she revealed the horrible secret that she only appeared to be a beautiful woman, but actually was a horrible skeleton, and all the villagers were like her, half-dead victims of a plague. The Worm Cult had just stolen the soul gem array that contained their spirits, and planed to use it to enslave them. William performed a ritual, offering a soul totem to Clavicus Vile, a prince of the supernatural entities inhabiting Oblivion, called the Daedra, and was transformed into a skeleton himself. In that form he infiltrated the Worm Cult, retrieved the stolen soul gem array, and returned to Chieftain Suhlak.

She then gave him the task of ultimate arbiter: "Preserve the soul gem array and we remain as we are, in this state between life and death. Destroy it and you end the curse, allowing us a final rest." Under the principles of Life Insurance, he had no choice but to preserve the gem and thus the village of skeletons, by placing it in the Ice of Stasis. Had he placed it in the Fires of Destruction, some of the skeletons would have attacked him. But either way, he would henceforth possess the Gemstone of Skeletal Visage that could disguise him as a skeleton.[5]

The main mission arc

During the hundred hours I ran William through *Elder Scrolls Online*, he performed many, many missions, a goodly fraction of which involving

DOI: 10.1057/9781137490599.0011

rescuing members of a questgiver's family, or sadly often only retrieving a memento from a corpse, comparable to the payoff from a life insurance policy. Fittingly, many missions required battling fire. The main quest line, running all the way to level 50, also involved rescues, beginning with "Daughter of Giants," a title that referred to Lyris Titanborn. The Prophet summoned William to The Harborage, a secret hideout they would use from that time onward, calling him *Vestige*, because he was the soulless remnant of a human being. William was not sure he had lost his soul, or had even possessed one, but he certainly seemed to have lost memories.

The Prophet helped William walk through visions of the past to understand better his own destiny, explaining, "The prophecies of the Elder Scrolls are a fluid, living thing. They are not fixed. At many points throughout history, the actions of heroic mortals have rewritten them." He spoke of Five Companions, a team of heroes who sought a magical artifact, The Amulet of Kings, and the main quest arc would require rescuing them, gaining the amulet, and along the way regaining William's own soul. Lyris Titanborn was one of the five, and the others were Varen Aquilarios, Abnur Tharn, Sai Sahan, and Mannimarco whose treachery opened a rift through which the demons of Oblivion could invade Tamriel. It seemed that Mannimarco had become leader of the Worm Cult, and thus many of William's miscellaneous missions were also insurance against the evils Mannimarco had unleashed.

When William reached level 10 of experience, The Prophet recalled him to The Harborage and announced that it was time to rescue Lyris Titanborn from Coldharbour. The Prophet opened a portal that teleported William there, and he easily reached Lyris, so the mission seemed trivially easy. But then she explained that fragments of her identity had been locked away in different places. Battling their way, the pair retrieved four fragments, each of which assuaged one portion of her distress: regret, solitude, uncertainty, and terror. Safely reaching The Harborage, William engaged Lyris in conversation, hoping she would reveal that her true identity was Simsey. The best she offered was vague words of encouragement: "I know it sounds strange … I knew you would come. I had faith in you. I still do. I hope we can be good friends."

Knowing that the next arc mission, "Chasing Shadows," could be difficult, William did it at level 17 rather than 15, gaining a magic orb that could help them find Sai Sahan, and communicating with the spirit of Abnur Tharn who had become the assistant to vile Mannimarco. At level 20, William was impatient, so he returned to The Harborage, from

DOI: 10.1057/9781137490599.0011

where he and Lyris would enter "Castle of the Worm" to rescue Abnur Tharn, who was prepared to renounce Mannimarco and help them find Sai Sahan. However, this mission ended with a horrendous battle, in which to his vast embarrassment he was defeated, thus shamed before Lyris. Out of an abundance of caution, he did not return to complete the mission until level 30, easily freeing Abnur Tharn and returning Lyris to The Harborage. There Abnur Tharn shared not only what he knew of the whereabouts of Sai Sahan but also those of Varen Aquilarios, who was in fact The Prophet and ultimately responsible as the former emperor for the disaster that had struck the world. Thus, while William had wondered about the real identity of Lyris Titanborn, he had failed to consider the real identity of The Prophet. Lyris had known, of course, and apologized: "I'm sorry I lied to you. I ... I hope we can still be friends."

William immediately began the level-25 mission in the arc, "The Tharn Speaks," which gave them the final information required for the level-30 mission, "Halls of Torment," which he began at level 32. For that major challenge, William was required to select either Abnur Tharn or Lyris Titanborn as his partner, and he chose her in hopes that she now finally would reveal the truth about her own identity. Among the enemies they had to confront was a Doppelganger of Lyris, revealing that Sai Sahan has a passion for Lyris that she had not recognized. Once all of them were safe at The Harborage, she begged William to say nothing about that: "I just need time to sort it all out." She did not express fondness for either Sai or William, nor did she reveal herself to be Simsey.

"Valley of the Blades" and "Shadow of Sancre Tor" both involve battling Mannimarco, the member of the original five who had betrayed them and was now preparing to betray his master, Molag Bal, the Daedric Prince of Domination. This pair of missions ends with the death of Mannimarco, and capture of the Amulet of Kings. The final mission, "God of Schemes" will pit the team against Molag Bal, also called the Father of Vampires and God of Brutality, who seeks to destroy the barriers that protect Tamriel from Oblivion. But first must be completed the penultimate quest, "Council of the Five Companions." Oddly, this mission involved no action, but two serious decisions in which William refused to accept obligation that conflicted with his own primary goal of finding Simsey.

Vanquishing Mannimarco destroyed the Worm Cult, but also left the Five one member short. Sai Sahan praised William's accomplishments, and invited him to join the Five, thereby completing its pentagram.

DOI: 10.1057/9781137490599.0011

However, William would consider committing himself to a team only if Simsey were a member of it, and he had come to doubt that Lyris Titanborn was in fact Simsey's avatar. The game offered William two choices: "I am honored to join you as the last member of the Five Companions." "The Five Companions failed. Let's not risk repeating history." He chose not to repeat a history of failure.

Abnur Tharn then explained that in fact the final mission would sacrifice one of the Five, because a human soul was required for a ritual required for success. Since Abner would perform the ritual, and William supposedly lacked a soul, neither of them could provide the self-sacrifice. In the final mission, William would be asked to decide which would be sacrificed: Varen Aquilarios, Sai Sahan, or Lyris Titanborn. Varen then gave William the opportunity to complete "Council of the Five Companions" and receive a magic ring, the Band of the Companions. He declined. Destroying Molag Bal could save thousands of lives, but William could not agree to sacrifice one life in the process.

A long conversation with Lyris Titanborn ended William's exploration of *Elder Scrolls Online*. She talked about friendship, yet did not sound like Simsey, who was bright, often gesturing, with many facial expressions. Lyris spoke of being unsuited to become a housewife, and spoke of having children mere as "Squeeze out a few whelps." She spoke of exploring the vast virtual world: "Traveling is a humbling experience. You see first hand what a small place you occupy in the world. Funny thing is, the farther you go, the harder it is to return. But when you do ... if you do ... you get to see the place you came from with new eyes."

Conclusion

My father would not have recognized the last words of Lyris Titanborn as a reference to T. S. Elliot: "We shall not cease from exploration, and the end of all our exploring will be to arrive where we started and know the place for the first time."[6] Could that have been Simsey whispering to him from the beyond? We shall never know. His refusal to join the Five and complete the main quest arc reflected a fundamental contradiction: Over the entire course of his 100 hours, saving a few virtual people had required killing hundreds of others. Even though the mathematics would be reversed in the final mission, completing it would amount to endorsement of the entire death-oriented system. Yes, WWB had

DOI: 10.1057/9781137490599.0011

called his profession "death insurance," but he really wanted it to be life insurance.

Notes

1 www.friendsseminary.org/podium/default.aspx?t=141496.
2 Viviana Zelizer, "Human Values and the Market: The Case of Life Insurance and Death in 19th Century America ." *American Journal of Sociology*, 1978, 84: 591–610.
3 Linda Pickthorne Fletcher, "Motivations Underlying the Mutualization of Stock Life Insurance Companies." *The Journal of Risk and Insurance*, 1966, 33(1): 19–32; Richard Spiller, "Ownership and Performance: Stock and Mutual Life Insurance Companies." *The Journal of Risk and Insurance*, 1972, 39(1): 17–25; David Mayers and Clifford W. Smith, Jr., "Executive Compensation in the Life Insurance Industry." *The Journal of Business*, 1992, 65(1): 51–74; Vivian Jeng, Gene C. Lai, and Michael J. McNamara, "Efficiency and Demutualization: Evidence from the U.S. Life Insurance Industry in the 1980s and 1990s." *The Journal of Risk and Insurance*, 2007, 74(3): 683–711.
4 William Sims Bainbridge, *eGods* (New York: Oxford University Press, 2013), pp. 167–170.
5 teso.mmorpg-life.com/quests/the-bargains-end/.
6 T. S. Eliot, *Four Quartets* (Orlando, FL: Harvest, 1943), p 240.

DOI: 10.1057/9781137490599.0011

10
Resting in Peace (*Lord of the Rings Online*)

Abstract: *This chapter seeks an antidote to despair, basing the avatar on the daughter of the couple memorialized in the two previous chapters, whose death with them came after a downward spiral when it seemed every problem that humans can experience afflicted her, one after another. Thus, this chapter shares some intimate details of her agonizing decline with respect for her courage, and following the principle that we need to admit the real horrors of human life before we can even begin to transcend them. The New Paradigm theory of religion analyzes faith in terms of* consolation, *experiencing a fictional solution to a real problem, thereby gaining psychological compensation for emotional distress. Here, three facts of her real life combine to determine that the appropriate MMO was* Lord of the Rings Online: *(1) She loved amateur theater, but was prevented by disabilities from becoming an actress. (2) She loved the popular music of her era. (3) She was assisted during one of her tragedies by a fiction she created in partnership with an uncle, who happened to be a close friend and colleague of J. R. R. Tolkien, the author of the* Lord of the Rings.

Bainbridge, William Sims. *An Information Technology Surrogate for Religion: The Veneration of Deceased Family in Online Games.* New York: Palgrave MacMillan, 2014.
DOI: 10.1057/9781137490599.0012.

Consolation: Experiencing a fictional solution to a real problem, thereby gaining psychological compensation for emotional distress.

This conclusion completes the exploration of how deceased persons can symbolically live again, by offering Barbara Constance Bainbridge (1943–1965) the opportunity to experience *Lord of the Rings Online* (LotRO), a realm very closely connected to Connie's real life, with an emphasis on every-day living more than adventuring. Earlier, I told part of her personal history in a collection of autobiographical essays by leading sociologists of religion.[1] I share it here with respect for her courage, and following the principle that we need to admit the real horrors of human life before we can even begin to transcend them.

Beyond belief

When news reached me of my sister's death, I was visiting in the home of our uncle Angus McIntosh (1914–2005) in Edinburgh, Scotland, a student and close friend of J. R. R. Tolkien, author of *The Hobbit* and the *Lord of the Rings* trilogy.[2] In 1952 Angus founded the Institute for Historical Dialectology at the University of Edinburgh, which today is called the Angus McIntosh Centre for Historical Linguistics.[3] Lacking even a gram of religious faith, I dealt with the horror by visiting pre-Christian ruins, including the Antonine Wall as well as Hadrian's Wall, which marked the temporary limits of the long-dead Roman Empire. At the Culloden battlefield, Angus showed me the mass grave of his clan, and at Urquhart Castle on Loch Ness we joked that an inch-long slug might be a baby of the mythical monster alleged to dwell in the deep waters. Later, I stood beside the heelstone at Stonehenge and contemplated what science had learned since the ancients first wondered about the heavens. Yet my primary reaction came the instant I learned what had happened to Connie: "Of course, this had to happen."

The last third of her life was filled with sadness, disappointment, and pain, for which neither religion nor science offered effective remedies. At adolescence, she developed epilepsy, although somehow her mother prevented her from ever knowing the name of her own disease, under the theory that it was too shameful to acknowledge. Each day she would experience several *petit mal* episodes in which her conscious mind briefly

DOI: 10.1057/9781137490599.0012

ceased to function, even as her more automatic functions continued. She began having rare but intense grand mal seizures, falling to the floor and shaking violently, then remaining semi-conscious for several minutes afterward. She could injure herself in a grand mal, but even the petit mals were dangerous, for example if one came on while she was walking across a street.

Her condition seemed perfect proof that the human soul was an illusion, merely a complex dynamic pattern of data based in the neuronal structure of the brain. I do not believe I ever heard her question the tenants of Christian religion, but nor did I see evidence that she took comfort from it. Rather, the church was part of her social environment, and she relied upon adults to organize the religious activities of her life. Her mother privately did not believe the doctrines of Christianity, but considered church membership to be a mark of social status in the community. Her father was not so cynical, treating religious faith as a form of honest loyalty to his family heritage, occasionally praying, but not apparently relying upon religion for encouragement. Around 1960, surprisingly Connecticut still had a eugenics law that technically would have prevented marriage of an epileptic, although a local Episcopal clergyman promised he would ignore this and perform a marriage ceremony when Connie was ready. Yet Connie's mother became angry at the church when she was unable to convince an Episcopal boarding school to admit her daughter, who in consequence of her disability was forced to leave the public school system. Perhaps some religious people could find solace in a theological explanation for debilitating epilepsy, but this family was never offered a plausible sacred antidote to despair.

Science proved a very imperfect substitute for religion. Medications did reduce the symptoms, but not cure the disease, and they had severe side effects. Most shockingly, Connie was among that small minority of patients taking paramethadione who suffered kidney failure, and she nearly died, especially given that dialysis was still in its infancy and was not locally available. Mysteriously, she suffered numerous nonmalignant fibroid tumors, most unfortunately on the bottom of her feet, which made standing difficult. She earned a cosmetology certificate and got a job at the Village Pharmacy in Old Greenwich, a tribute to the benevolence of the proprietors, living for a time in a boarding house with hope that she could be independent in adulthood. However, among the side effects of the medication were that she could not wake herself up in the morning. So a depressed but decent fellow resident with a night watch-man job would wake her every morning when he returned from work, until the day he swallowed a bottle of her pills and after a month in a coma, died.

Both religion and science provide some benefits for humanity, yet lack the ability to achieve real salvation. Family and community have their own limitations, and even in combination all human institutions fall far short of being panaceas. At one point Connie was engaged to be married, and perhaps too aggressively her mother put announcements in the newspapers, but the man's mother apparently convinced him suddenly to break off communications just before the happy day, adding one more severe trauma to the growing disaster. Exploited by a man she met at the tavern she frequented, she came to believe she was again engaged to be married, and began wearing one of her mother's rings as if it were evidence of her engagement. Then the man proved her wrong by hurling the ring into bushes where it could not be found, leaving her pregnant and in despair.

The last weeks of the pregnancy were spent in hiding in Tarrytown, New York, while pretending to be in Edinburgh, Scotland. Connie had indeed visited Edinburgh years before, with her mother, but now to prevent her self-righteous community from learning about her preg-nancy, her parents conspired with Angus McIntosh to authenticate a cover story that she was visiting him across the ocean on an innocent vacation. Angus bought many Edinburgh postcards, and mailed them in a package to Connie. She wrote little messages about her fictitious tourism, addressed the cards to her friends, and sent the package back to Angus. He then affixed British postage stamps and mailed them on her behalf.

Exhausted by these agonizing events, she retreated to her parent's home where death awaited her. Her motto during this time was, "At least you know you're living!" After a dark night lit by horrible flames, she could no longer say those words. One local newspaper revealed the scandal of her secret pregnancy, exploiting her sad story as if it were a soap opera rather than profound tragedy, and others published pictures of the half-burned home where her life had ended. How much of ordi-nary human life is fundamentally unreal, I cannot say, yet the incident of pretending to be in Scotland added plausibility that she could be virtu-ally resurrected inside the fantasy world created by the mentor of her uncle, J. R. R. Tolkien.

DOI: 10.1057/9781137490599.0012

Entering Middle Earth

The land called *Middle Earth*, inhabited by Hobbits and Elves as well as Humans, has many, many meanings. Family tradition actually holds that Angus was the model for the Hobbits, and the online Tolkien encyclopedia gives some credence to this legend.[4] There exist several radically different interpretations of Middle Earth, including most plausibly that it is an English translation of *Midgard*, the realm where old Norse, Germanic, and Anglo-Saxon legends took place. Equally obvious, but engendering endless debates, is the parallel between Tolkien's *Lord of the Rings* and Richard Wagner's *Ring of the Nibelung*. Each is a vast mythology about the ancient world but serving as a critique of the modern world. Each is a tetralogy, in which the first of four parts is simpler than the other three. Each concerns a supernatural conflict in which a magical ring confers power to the individual who holds it, but danger to all humanity, ending with the return of that ring to nature and the end of a dynasty of supernatural beings.

Traumatized by the loss of friends in the First World War, then watching the Second World War entangle Wagner in the ideology of the enemy, Tolkien may have intended the ring to represent the dangers of advanced technology. He is reported to have opposed innovations such as spaceflight, which after all was a development arising from the Nazi side in the Second World War.[5] Clearly, his writings look to the humane past for inspiration, not the technical future. In a very real sense, he was a reincarnation of Snorri Sturluson, an Icelandic historian who lived seven centuries earlier. While a Christian, Sturluson sought to preserve, retell, and analyze the pre-Christian legends of his people.[6] Tolkien did the same thing for the ancient English legends, except that since many of them had been lost—erased by the Christians one might charge—he invented some. As a devout Roman Catholic, Tolkien managed to structure his story around the catholic principle that all peoples of the world should come together in a single fellowship, yet strenuously avoided any direct reference to Christianity, such as setting a scene in a cathedral.[7]

Released in April 2007, LotRO is one of the very highest quality MMOs, by any measure. I had studied it back in 2009, through a main character named Rumilisoun, whom I imagined was the grand-daughter of the Elf named Rúmil, whom Tolkien said had invented the art of writing. Something of a pedant, she actually published an essay under her own name in a leading computer science periodical.[8] At the time, the top

DOI: 10.1057/9781137490599.0012

experience level in LotRO was 65, and I took Rumilisoun that high. But I had a second character, a Hobbit named Angusmcintosh, who refused to leave the Shire where his little people lived, and never went above level 20. Thus I could well imagine that Connie had been invited by Angus to visit him in Middle Earth.

But there were in fact many Middle Earths, which is to say, multiple Internet servers, and I decided that the one where Rumilisoun and Angus dwelt was not the right one, even as I decided that "Connie" would not be the right name for her to use. In real life, Connie had participated in amateur theater, first the Summer Youth Festival whose early rehearsals were hosted at the Congregational Church in Old Greenwich, then performed in the auditorium at Riverside Junior High School. Later she joined a more adult group, the Connecticut Playmakers. Her health problems brought an end to her involvement, but now imagining her restored to perfect health, I believe she would have loved role-playing in *Lord of the Rings*, so I selected the primary English role-playing server, Laurelin.

But she would have used a name other than her own, as actresses always do in the theater. I decided that she should use an Anglo-Saxon version of her formal name, Constance, and settled on Ánræda. An online dictionary says that one meaning of *ánræd* is *constant*, others being: of one mind, unanimous, firm, persevering, and resolute.[9] Ánræda would be a Human character, rather than an Elf like Rumilisoun, a fact that determined where she would enter Middle Earth and what she would experience in her first ten levels of progress.

She awoke in a prison cell, just as Strider came to rescue her. He was a ranger of the north, a prominent hero throughout the *Rings* books, whose real name was Aragorn. I decided that his real mission was to rescue Constance from the prison that had been her epilepsy, and liberate her to become Ánræda or whatever she might have wished. Soon she freed Hobbit captives who set the prison complex afire, to distract its guards, and I was forced to contemplate whether fire could ever be a liberator rather than a destroyer.

After their escape, Ánræda found herself in a peaceful town called Archet, inhabited by both Humans and Hobbits, and the tutorial training ground for characters belonging to these two races. Ánræda was not initially free to leave Archet, but was required to perform a variety of missions up to level 8 of experience, learning the necessary skills to function in LotRO, as well as some of the background lore. Then a terrible

DOI: 10.1057/9781137490599.0012

attack set the town aflame, and once again she needed to survive a fire, after which she was able to leave the area and decide for herself what her fate would be.

Seeking kinship

By level 10 of experience, Ánræda had reached The Prancing Pony, the tavern in the large town of Bree that was the center of LotRO social life, where she chatted with other players and contemplated what she might do with her restored life. Much of Connie's social life had been centered on taverns in Port Chester, New York, where the drinking age was 18 compared with 21 in her home town of Greenwich across the border in Connecticut. She especially frequented Vahsen's, which subsequently entered the mythology of rock music when Janis Joplin reputedly wrote her last song there. Now, at The Prancing Pony, she sipped an ale, enjoyed the music, and overheard conversations like this one:

> Chivo says, "Oh, I love this tune. Muh grammy used t' play this song and tell me stories of a dark, secretive forest and a kind ol' man who watched over it."
> Leeko says, "Yer nan was quite an interestin' lady, Chivo' … 'good stories, she had! Lots of em' too!"
> Chivo says, "Aye, that she did!"
> Chivo says, "Eh, who's that lovely elf over there? Quite a looka', eh?"
> Leeko says, "Chivo, mind yourself. People can hear yer gabberin'"
> Chivo says, "*clears throat* Yes, righto. *blushes*" [He now notices a tall, female Human at the entrance.]
> Zurich leans against the doorframe, gazing out at the inn. The air was pleasant and fun this evening, it seemed, and she'll allow herself a small smile, for it would be a good change.
> Chivo bows deeply before Zurich.
> Chivo says, "Shame for a lady like yourself be alone on a night like this."
> Zurich quirks a grin down to the hobbit, not returning the bow. She'll snort as he says this. "Aye, ain't it?"
> Chivo blushes crimson red.
> Chivo says, "Well.. um.. how are you?"
> Zurich seems amused, peering down at him through her hood and mask. "I can't complain. An' yerself, small man?"
> Chivo says, "I just saw you over here, all by yourself and …. Oh, I'm well, thank ye."
> Chivo says, "Well, I was just wonderin'" if ye felt like "avin' a drink."
> Zurich says, "I'll … Hava' tea, if ya' please. Yer too kind."

DOI: 10.1057/9781137490599.0012

Chivo, Leeko, and Zurich were characters used for role-playing, as if they were real residents of Bree, socializing in a real local tavern. This conversation began around 8:30 in the evening, April 13, 2014. Chivo and Leeko were both Hobbit men, only at level 7 and probably created just for role-playing at the tavern, while Zurich was a level-20 female "Man," but Tolkien used this term for Humans of both genders. Ánræda wondered what it would be like to have a Hobbit boyfriend, imagining she could dominate one because of his small stature. Ánræda saw that Zurich was of the sneaky burglar class, and belonged to a kinship with the worrisome name, Indignation.

Ánræda had found safety, but not yet meaning. I opened the biography section of the interface, where players conceptualize their characters, and wrote: "Oh, the flames! The choking smoke! Our home seemed so safe, on Lucas Point, even when the storms poured water into our road, separated as we were from the conflicts of the wider world. When my health declined, I retreated back home to rest, hopefully to recuperate, but not to die. Then the fire burned away all hopes. Yet here I live again! What can it all possibly mean?"

Perhaps poetry could provide meaning. A poetry festival was advertised for the following weekend at a Hobbit gathering place called Bywater. Lucas Point was certainly by the water, and Hurricane Carol had flooded the streets in 1954. On April 19, 2014, Ánræda sat on the soft grass at Hobbiton-Bywater, listening to poets recite their works, such as the following melancholy lines by a Hobbit lady named Lina, who must have known much struggle and strife, since she had reached the maximum current experience level of 95:

> With rain and sleet and drizzling drops, the seeds began ter sprout
> The finest garden in the Shire, of that I had no doubt.
> The harvest would be grand this year, the flowers rich and strong,
> But nature soon resolved ter prove me dreams were naught but wrong.

The many lines that followed in Lina's long poem, and the other poets after Lina, seemed deceptively simple, expressing deep feeling about life in often colloquial language. Ánræda felt drawn to these Hobbits, and repelled by the combat that would be required to reach level 95 as Lina had done. She resolved to settle down, with whatever modest experience was required to achieve a secure and happy life.

On April 27. Ánræda returned to the Hobbit Shire, beside a waterfall in the distant Delving Fields, to attend a concert by a band of five Hobbits

DOI: 10.1057/9781137490599.0012

called the Songburrow Strollers who belonged to the Grand Order of the Lost Mathom kinship. The word *mathom* is sometimes translated as treasure or gift, but a *Lord of the Rings* wiki says, "Mathom was the hobbit term for anything which they had no use for but were unwilling to throw away."[10] Wiktionary notes that it is really an Anglo-Saxon word, properly spelled *maþum*.[11] So the Hobbits spoke Ánræda's own native language. And for her, life itself was a mathom, possibly valueless but precious.

She wished she could join the Songburrow Strollers, but they seemed very hobbity, and in stature if not spirit she towered high above them. She checked the website of their kinship, reading this description of the group: "The Grand Order of the Lost Mathom (more often known simply as The Grand Order or The Order), are a primarily scholarly society dedicated to the preservation, collection and further understanding of mathoms. Their members are also concerned with keeping alive the traditions of storytelling, poetry and song through study, research, performances and lectures."[12]

At one point in the concert she inspected the information available about the five performers. Nimelia, a level-88 guardian, was playing the flute, while a horn was in the hands of Tibba Stoutfoot, a level-89 minstrel. Another minstrel named Sevelda Quickkettle, at level 85, banged a hand drum, while a level-91 guardian named Simbo Rumblebelly, the only male on the band, strummed a huge theorbo, a lute-type instrument even larger than an arch lute. The leader, who stood in the center, was level-95 warden, Lina Willowwood. She had composed the theme song for the band, The Strollers' Waltz, which begins:

> One day in the Shire I'll never forget
> A band of musicians out playing I met
> They belted out songs and spread joy on their way
> The Songburrow Strollers are playing today[13]

At the peak of the concert, 28 avatars were gathered at the waterfall: 1 dwarf, 2 humans counting Ánræda herself, 3 Elves, and 22 Hobbits who were all wearing pointy green hats. For a while Ánræda listened to the music while sitting on the grass, then she stood and clapped her hands, then she danced. Looking at the few tall people at the concert she discovered they were all members of a kinship called The Order of the White Flame. If they, like she, were drawn to the Hobbit concert, maybe they were of like minds, and she should join them. Seeing that one of the Elves, named Aifel, was a level-95 minstrel, she asked him

DOI: 10.1057/9781137490599.0012

if it might be possible to join his kinship. He politely introduced her to the group's leader who also had attended the concert, a level-95 guard named Trincia who was herself a Hobbit, but wearing an elegant white gown with no pointy green hat. A few moments later, Ánræda was a member of The Order of the White Flame, which indeed turned out to be the ideal kinship for her.

A performance in Bree

When she joined the White Flames, Ánræda was only level 11 and had no motivation to ascend higher. But if she was going to master all the musical instruments, she would need to get at least to level 15, when she could play a theorbo, and level 25, when she would gain the bagpipes skill, which seemed necessary given the partial Scottish ancestry of Connie. She knew that her mother's family, Sims, was a division of the Fraser clan, and owned a kilt with the proper tartan.[14] Still only at level 12, on Friday, May 2, she went for the first time to the mansion that served as the kinship's headquarters, at 8 Haven Way in Falathorn Homesteads. It was marvelous, as documented by a trophy in the front yard, announcing that it was the best house in the neighborhood. Trincia arrived with four other members, then staged a brief ceremony on a small outdoor stage that promoted Ánræda to kinswoman rank. In what follows, "[Kinship] Trincia:" means that Trincia is speaking in the kinship text chat that all six avatars present can read. "[To Kinship]" means that Ánræda herself is speaking in that chat. "Trincia tells you," means that Trincia is speaking in a private text chat to Ánræda, which others cannot read. Statements like "You kneel" refer to actions taken by avatars, among which bowing and cheering are called *emotes* because they express emotions:

[Kinship] Trincia: Anraeda, please step forward
[Kinship] Trincia: Anraeda, you have been a recruit our kinship Order of the
    White Flame for some time. Would you do us the honour of becoming a
    resident member of our kinship?
[To Kinship] Indeed, it would be an honor.
Trincia tells you, "When I say please present me your weapon paste in the
    following: /me presents his weapon to Trincia"
[Kinship] Trincia: Anraeda, please present me your weapon.
Trincia tells you, "Make a swordsalute by doing the emote /swordsalute or /
    salute."
Anraeda presents her weapon to Trincia

DOI: 10.1057/9781137490599.0012

Trincia tells you, "After I tell you to kneel and swear the oath, do the emote /
kneel and paste in the following:"
You salute smartly.
Trincia tells you, "I place an oath from my heart upon this weapon, that I will
be true to the values of the Order. This includes kindness, honour, trust
and loyalty to those within the kinship. I shall treat everyone as an equal
and will never tarnish the name of the order."
[Kinship] Trincia: Anraeda, kneel and swear the oath on your weapon!
You kneel.
[To Kinship] I place an oath from my heart upon this weapon, that I will be
true to the values of the Order. This includes kindness, honour, trust and
loyalty to those within the kinship. I shall treat everyone as an equal and
will never tarnish the name of the order.
[Kinship] Trincia: Anraeda, I now promote you to kinsman in Order of the
White Flame.
A new title has been bestowed upon you, you may now be known as Anraeda,
Kinswoman!
You have been promoted to Kinswoman by Trincia.
Nallen cheers at Anraeda.
Trincia bows deeply before Anraeda.
Arsamwen cheers at Anraeda.
Brinhelm cheers at Anraeda.
You bow.
Gwathelwen cheers at Anraeda.
Trincia cheers at Anraeda.

After the ceremony, they toured the elegant interior of the mansion, and
they discussed a rehearsal the band might have the following Sunday.
I scrambled to get Ánræda ready, advancing her to level 15, copying musical arrangements by Trincia and Aifel in the "ABC" notation
system that controlled the LotRO music synthesizer, and downloading
from the Web an "add-on" program called Songbook that could manage
communications so that an orchestra with many parts could play in a
coordinated manner.[15] Seven band members showed up, and despite the
great complexity of the system, Ánræda was successfully able to play first
a clarinet, then switch to a flute, then a lute. This took a good deal of skill
with computer interfaces, but not actual musical skill, because the music
synthesizer in the LotRO software produced all the sounds, including
coordinating the instruments on the user's machine. The player operating Trincia was in Sweden, most players were in other areas of Western

DOI: 10.1057/9781137490599.0012

Europe, while one player was in New Orleans, and Ánræda's player was in Arlington, Virginia. That meant that delays would have confused the music, had the system attempted to assemble the sounds anywhere other than the user's machine.

Given the success of the rehearsal, Trincia scheduled a public performance for May 11, with the stipulation that band members must wear specific elegant uniforms, which for the women would mean a gossamer dress that could be obtained only from an NPC cosmetics vendor at a skirmish camp. LotRO, like many other MMOs, has multiple forms of money, and the vendor would require a payment of 149 marks for a gossamer dress, but Ánræda had only 60, acquired from completing some odd missions. That meant she had to complete missions for the quest-giver at the skirmish camp, which were special missions in separate instanced environments, and required reaching level 20. After rushing to level 20, Ánræda did the introductory skirmish missions, which taught her the procedures, and had her defend The Prancing Pony in the absence of any other avatars. She earned some marks, reaching a total of 141, just short of her goal, so she completed a different skirmish, holding 154 marks when she bought the dress. She was level 25 and possessed a full collection of instruments, when the band assembled at the kinship's headquarters for a last minute rehearsal on May 11.

Ten members of the band gathered outside The Prancing Pony in Bree: Trincia, Aifel, Nallen, Brinhelm, Lynith, Finsamidor, Gwathelwen, Grimfax, Nilgo, and Ánræda. They stood on a grassy area, as an audience gathered, some attracted by advertisements Trincia had sent out, and others noticing that something was happening at the very center of LotRO social activity. Over an hour and a half, beginning at three in the afternoon Eastern US time, but mid-evening European time, they played 20 tunes, beginning and ending with "Theme of The White Flame." The audience varied as avatars came and went, but often approached 20. Some stood, some sat, and others danced. The music was truthfully of a sort Connie loved, and I am sure she knew these tunes: "Mack the Knife" dating from 1928, "Body and Soul" from 1930, "Porgy and Bess" from 1935, and "Nice Work if You Can Get It" from 1937. She would not have heard, "You Are the Sunshine of My Life" from 1973, having died eight years earlier, but now, I imagined, she played it with intense feeling.

DOI: 10.1057/9781137490599.0012

Conclusion

For all I know, Ánræda could outlive me, if LotRO continues, and a sympathetic soul inherits the password for the account she is on. But for this book project, her tour of duty ended on August 17, 2014. She played in the band one more time, when the White Flames performed the music of Frank Zappa, whose first album was released only the year after she died. An advertisement on the role-playing website for the Laurelin server showed a picture of the May 11 performance, with Ánræda in the center playing lute, and proclaimed: "The Order of the White Flame, an entrepreneurial group of Elves, Men, Hobbits and Dwarves, bound together by the desire to restore Hope to Middle Earth where it is needed most, are holding a free concert for the Citizens of Bree during this dark time. Join them for this unique and original performance the likes of which has never been seen, and enjoy the show."[16] Is hope needed most in Middle Earth, or in the Earth we physically inhabit, wracked by political discord, economic chaos, and religious doubt? Whatever the state of the world may be, at any moment many people experience a "dark time," ending in total darkness. We can wonder what alternatives to traditional religion may be provided to future generations by information technology.

Notes

1 William Sims Bainbridge, "Stranger in a Strange Land," in *Studying Religion and Society: Sociological Self-Portraits*, edited by Titus Hjelm and Phil Zuckerman (London: Routledge, 2013), pp. 26–38.

2 J. R. R. Tolkien, *The Lord of the Rings* (London: Allen and Unwin, 1955).

3 www.ppls.ed.ac.uk/lel/groups/angus-mcintosh-centre-for-historical-linguistics, accessed June 10, 2014.

4 tolkiengateway.net/wiki/Angus_McIntosh.

5 Arthur C. Clarke, *Voices from the Sky* (New York: Harper, 1965), p. 175.

6 Snorri Sturluson, *The Prose Edda* (New York: Oxford University Press, 1916).

7 Humphrey Carpenter, *J. R. R. Tolkien: A Biography* (Boston, MA: Houghton Mifflin, 1977).

8 Rumilisoun, "Rebirth of Worlds," *Communications of the ACM*, 2010, 53(12): 128.

9 www.oldenglishtranslator.co.uk/.

10 lotr.wikia.com/wiki/Mathom.

DOI: 10.1057/9781137490599.0012

11   en.wiktionary.org/wiki/ma%C3%BEum#Old_English.

12   lostmathom.org/pages/about/4.

13   lostmathom.org/threads/songbook.355/.

14   www.rampantscotland.com/clans/blclanfraser.htm.

15   lotro-wiki.com/index.php/Music, www.lotrointerface.com/downloads/
      info380-Songbook.html.

16   laurelinarchives.org/node/260444.

DOI: 10.1057/9781137490599.0012